MEDICATION, NON-COMPLIANCE AND MENTALLY DISORDERED OFFENDERS

THE ROLE OF NON-COMPLIANCE IN HOMICIDE BY PEOPLE WITH MENTAL ILLNESS AND PROPOSALS FOR FUTURE POLICY

A STUDY OF INDEPENDENT INQUIRY REPORTS

BY

MICHAEL HOWLETT
DIRECTOR OF THE ZITO TRUST

ISBN 1 900252 10 4

CONTENTS

THE ZITO TRUST

RESEARCH PROGRAMME

Introduction

Since The Zito Trust was established in July 1994 (it was registered as a charity in January 1995), its activities have focused on three discrete but complementary areas of work. These are:

- ***providing support*** and advice to a wide range of people who contact the Trust and who have suffered in some way as a result of the failure or breakdown of community care for the severely mentally ill

- ***campaigning for change*** by lobbying parliament; by raising awareness through the media and the Trust's own new journal *ZT Monitor*, and by keeping abreast of developments in the mental health field

- ***undertaking research*** in vital areas of service provision and practice

The Research Programme

The Zito Trust's research programme focuses mainly on the independent inquiries into homicide committed by mentally ill people. These inquiries contain a wealth of information and recommendations about mental health services. Research activity by The Zito Trust on the inquiries already completed and published, and proposals for the future, include:

- *Learning The Lessons: Mental Health Inquiry Reports published in England and Wales between 1969 and 1996 and their recommendations for improving practice.* (Two editions, 1995 & 1996)

- *Community Care Homicides Since 1990.* (October 1997)

- *Medication, Non-Compliance and Mentally Disordered Offenders: The Role of Non-Compliance in Homicide by People with Mental Illness and Proposals for Future Policy.* (April 1998)

- *Lessons to be Learned about Risk: A Study of the Independent Inquiries.* (due 1999)

- *Mental Disorder and Violent Behaviour: A Review of the Literature.* (due 1999)

Financial assistance

The Zito Trust would like to thank the Department of Health for the award of a Section 64 Grant which helps finance the support service offered by the Trust. For their financial assistance in support of our research programme, the Trust would like to thank The Allen Lane Foundation, The Baily Thomas Charitable Fund, The Calouste Gulbenkian Foundation, The Dunhill Medical Trust, The Hayward Foundation, Lundbeck Limited and The Sir Samuel Scott of Yews Trust.

MEDICATION, NON-COMPLIANCE AND MENTALLY DISORDERED OFFENDERS

EXECUTIVE SUMMARY

This report is a study of homicides committed by mentally ill people who were receiving treatment from mental health services and whose non-compliance with medication was subsequently considered to have been a major contributory factor in the breakdown of care leading to the homicide. The evidence concerning non-compliance and its consequences is taken from the published independent inquiry reports into the care and treatment of individual patients who went on to commit homicide. Because non-compliance with medication should not be considered as an isolated feature of care, the report looks at a number of other issues, including the factors which influence non-compliance, the standard of care provided in individual cases, and some of the recommendations for improving compliance with treatment. The report also presents a study of statistics currently available on the number of homicides committed by mentally ill people, the relationship between mental illness and violence, and treatment in the absence of consent. The report also questions whether discussion of these and other issues increases stigmatisation of the mentally ill by the general public. Finally, there is a brief review of recent developments in the medical treatment of schizophrenia. Highlights from the report include the following:

- Twenty (57%) of the 35 homicide independent inquiry reports studied concerned patients whose non-compliance with medication in the community was revealed to be a major contributory factor in the breakdown of care before the homicide was committed. (Chapter 3)

- A number of factors influenced non-compliance in these 20 cases, including side-effects of the medication (85%), poor aftercare and supervision (85%), lack of insight by the patient (80%), substance abuse (65%), poor communication with the family and/or the patient (55%), and non-attendance by the patient at outpatient appointments (50%). (Chapter 5)

- It is estimated that over 70% of psychiatric patients discharged from hospital to the community will stop taking their prescribed medication within two years.

- Despite the availability of new drugs for the treatment of schizophrenia, with fewer side-effects, most patients are still being prescribed conventional drugs which have disabling side-effects. The reasons for this appear to be ignorance (clinicians not receiving information/training about the new drugs), and cost (the difference between £0.08 and £5.00 per day per patient). There is evidence to suggest that 'informal' health authority bans are in place in some areas, influencing prescribing practices on the basis of cost. (Chapter 8)

- Current Home Office homicide statistics do not enable commentators to give accurate figures for the number of homicides committed by mentally ill people. Estimates from the National Confidential Inquiry suggest that 43% of homicides are committed by people with a mental disorder of some kind, including alcohol/substance abuse and/or personality disorder; 25% are committed by people known to have had a history of contact with mental health services, and 12% by people who have had contact with the mental health services within the previous year. The total number of homicides for England and Wales in 1995 lies within the range of 518 (number convicted) and 663 (number currently recorded as homicide). (Chapter 6)

- The view still held by some people that the mentally ill are not more likely to commit crimes of violence than anyone else is incorrect. Research studies from a number of countries since the mid 1980s show significantly increased rates of violence among the mentally ill, particularly among people suffering from schizophrenia who are driven to offend by their delusions. Rates of violence increase by up to 17 times for males, and 85 times for females, where the diagnosis is schizophrenia and alcoholism. (Chapter 7)

- Research shows that the severely mentally ill are at risk of arming themselves as a rational response to irrational delusions. The independent homicide inquiries show that most of the victims were stabbed. (Chapter 7)

- The view that media attention devoted to homicide and violence by mentally disordered offenders increases stigmatisation of the mentally ill is not supported by the evidence. Research published by MORI in September 1997 shows that 72% of those members of the public asked felt that with careful support and modern medicines people with schizophrenia could live in the community. Only 12% said people with schizophrenia should live in institutions for the mentally ill. Only 18% said they would not be willing to work alongside someone with schizophrenia. The research conducted in 1997 shows an improvement in public attitudes towards the mentally ill over similar research carried out in 1990. (Introduction)

- New powers of supervised discharge to ensure that some categories of patient take their medication do not work and should be repealed. It is doubtful whether new legislation permitting treatment without consent in the community can be supported, or that it would work. A programme of training and education is urgently required on existing powers under the Mental Health Act 1983, and under criminal justice legislation, which are currently not utilised effectively by clinicians. (Chapter 2)

- Assertive outreach programmes with multidisciplinary teams supervising small groups of 10-15 patients should be implemented by every health authority and new funding must be made available to support these programmes, in addition to funding for new 24 hour nursed beds in every authority, and in addition to new funding to prescribe new treatments for schizophrenia. (Chapter 2)

- New services are urgently required to treat mentally ill people who suffer from alcohol and/or substance abuse. (Introduction, Chapter 5, Chapter 7)

INTRODUCTION

Community care : some of the current problems

The Zito Trust provides support and advice to a wide range of people who experience difficulties with community care for the mentally ill; from those who are bereaved by homicide and suicide, right the way through to people who ring up to express their concerns about neighbours who appear to them to be suffering from mental illness, who are behaving in an increasingly anti-social and sometimes threatening manner, yet who have apparently been abandoned by the system.

One such recent call is typical of many. A 50 year-old woman living at home in north London told us she is at the end of her tether. Her husband, who has been suffering from mental illness for seven years, has stopped taking his medication. His mental health is deteriorating and she feels that the whole family (three young children) are at risk. Her husband feels there is nothing wrong with him and refuses to go to his GP to collect his prescription. The medication, in tablet form, is for the treatment of depression and schizophrenia (amitriptyline, stelazine and procyclidine). His wife is no longer welcome in the marital bed and has to sleep every night on the sofa. He is communicating less and less, at least verbally. He has been arrested once, recently, for a breach of the peace following an incident at home when he refused to let his ten year-old leave the house to stay with an aunt. The police let him go without further ado. There have been threats of violence.

Before contacting The Zito Trust, the woman phoned social services and the local health centre. A social worker and a community psychiatric nurse arrived at the house the same day and attempted to talk to her husband. He was calm and plausible until he realised he was repeating himself, at which point he ordered the two visitors out of his house. The woman pleaded with them on the doorstep to do something. The community psychiatric nurse told her to ring the police if anything happened. They left with no promise to return. The husband is furious with his wife for making contact with the services in the first place. The situation she and her family are left in is worse than ever.

This kind of case is frustrating because it is so common. Nearly every call we take concerning the deterioration in someone's mental health has medication, and the refusal to take it any longer, as a significant element. There are, of course, other sociological and environmental elements which contribute just as much to the overall picture. Usually when people contact The Zito Trust the situation, if not grave, has reached such a stage where there are considerable anxieties, if not real fear. We will contact the relevant services on their behalf and express our concerns. In some cases something good comes out of it. More often than not, however, we end up advising people to write to their MPs. Meanwhile, time passes and things get worse, so we all cross our fingers and hope for the best.

Most of the cases where community care works least well concern families and neighbours. The difficulties families have include getting mental health professionals to take their concerns seriously. Quite often, the dynamics exhibited by families in distress, particularly in inner cities, are precisely the kinds of dynamics that professionals describe as a nightmare and will go out of their way to avoid. Engaging with a family in crisis requires a range of skills, particularly time and patience; skills which are in short supply in over-stretched and under-resourced services.

With an increasing number of hospital patients being accommodated in the community, we find we are getting numerous calls from the people living next door, above or below them. We have heard, informally, that the current Secretary of State for Health has an ex Whittington Hospital patient regularly climbing into his back garden, and is sick of it. This story may be apocryphal but has the ring of authenticity about it, given what we are dealing with at The Zito Trust. Health authorities close down hospitals, discharging patients into the care of local authority social services, which then pass them on to the voluntary sector, or to housing associations, to meet their accommodation needs. Many of them are housed in flats on their own and receive no face-to-face contact from the services from that point onwards. The idea that some friendly person on a bicycle is doing the rounds and imbibing capacious amounts of tea is arcadian, and has a wonderfully nostalgic feel about it, because that is, precisely, what many of these ex hospital patients need.

What generally happens instead? In far too many cases they become increasingly isolated and lonely, they have no friends, no employment and no occupational interests; they stop taking their medication and there is no one around to help them with their problems. Their mental state deteriorates and their lifestyles go downhill. Up goes the music late at night, followed by loud banging on the walls. The water upstairs is left on during the day, flooding the flat below. Rubbish is pushed through people's letter boxes, threats are made in response to psychotic delusions. A kitchen knife is left outside someone's front door. A man masturbates against a neighbour's garden fence. Someone's tyres are slashed, there is hysterical screaming in the street in the early hours of the morning.

If the psychosis deepens in a context like this, the chances of violence to self or others increases. When delusions become too powerful to cope with, a perfectly 'rational' response is to get rid of them, by an aggressive strike directed outwardly or inwardly.

The failure to provide therapeutic services contributes to much of this violence. Some of it ends in death, either of the self or of someone else. This report focuses on one aspect of care - medication - and the extent to which non-compliance with medication had a significant role in the circumstances leading to one particular and tragic consequence of community care failure, one which has been of considerable concern to our society in modern times, namely homicide committed by people who have been in contact with mental health services.

There are two reasons for focusing on non-compliance and homicide. The first concerns the way in which The Zito Trust was set up in 1994. Most people with an interest in this field know the background and the circumstances of Jonathan Zito's death in December 1992 and how, with the incident involving Ben Silcock in the lions' den at London Zoo, there was the first serious attention given to, and questions asked about, community care for the severely mentally ill. The unique nature of the organisation has meant that The Zito Trust has developed a special interest in homicide.

The second reason for focusing on non-compliance and homicide has to do with the availability of information about the subject contained in the independent inquiry reports into these cases since Jonathan Zito's death and the subsequent report of the inquiry into the treatment of the man who killed him, Christopher Clunis, which was published in February 1994. It would have been possible to look at the information gathered by The Zito Trust from the support service we offer, which would have involved considerably more examples of non-compliance which have not led to homicides. They have, in many cases, led to suicide, self-harm or harm to others, but the details are not in the public domain and we would have rendered ourselves liable to the claim that we were arguing our case anecdotally.

Community care : the ideology

'Did we ever dream, as we marched out of the asylums, that a few miles down the road we would have lost so much - budgets, integrated teams, expertise, facilities and morals - in the name of 'community psychiatry'? But it is our patients who will be the real losers if they are either neglected in the pseudo-community or re-institutionalised as a result of public backlash.'

Thus Robertson (1994) begins an article which is given the title 'Community psychiatry: weasel words?' This 'personal view' is of interest because it questions the use of terminology, suggests the abandonment of the expression 'community psychiatry' and a moratorium on its further use 'for at least a decade.' Dr Robertson, writing at a critical point in the 20 year local project with which he has been professionally involved to close down the old asylum and replace institutional care with a network of local community services, makes an interesting distinction between two sorts of 'community' found in German sociology. The first is *Gemeinschaft*, which implies an organic entity with 'cultural coherence'. The second is *Gesellschaft*, which is simply a 'collection of people sharing the same geographical space'. Which particular definition of 'community care' did our planners have in mind when they decided to close down the institutions?

It is difficult to tell, especially if one looks at experiences outside the UK. The leading ideological example of a pure socio-political response to institutionalisation, with its inherent idealisation of *Gemeinschaft*, took place in Italy in 1978, following inspired political lobbying dominated by left wing movements, of which *psychiatrica democratica* was the best known. Italian Law 180 effectively closed all public psychiatric hospitals throughout the country. The leading force for change was psychiatrist Franco Basaglia.

By the 1960s, when this mass social movement for change first found its voice, the accepted norms about mental illness had come under attack, not only in Italy but in the USA and UK. These norms included the belief that madness was a disease and a major social problem, a belief reinforced by psychiatrists, whose power was challenged as abusive and tyrannical. Campaigners using the law as their principle weapon sought to challenge these abuses of power, to protect the rights of the oppressed minority and to challenge the right of the 'therapeutic state' to take away an individual's civil liberties. The concept of mental illness was itself challenged, with intellectual forces coming from the right as well as the left of the political spectrum; Thomas Szasz and the Chicago School of Sociology, Foucault, Goffman, Laing and Cooper, to mention but a few of the thinkers who set reform in motion.

Part of the problem with the 'Italian Experience', as it came to be called, was the way in which influential organisations and individuals in other countries idealised it as the answer to all their prayers. Law 180 was passed in a country that had no meaningful experience of 'community care', it was driven by politics, and its focal point was Trieste where Franco Basaglia was a medical director. During the late 1970s Trieste, which is not typical of Italy in any case, had a huge housing surplus, enabling Basaglia to reduce the city's inpatient population by 60% in five years.

Housing helps. It is, of course, fundamental. When Basaglia tried to repeat the Trieste 'success' in Lazio he was very quickly brought down to earth, describing conditions there as 'catastrophic' and he died soon after.

Kathleen Jones, Emeritus Professor of Social Policy at York University, has reconsidered the 'Italian Experience' (Jones and Poletti, 1986). Touring psychiatric facilities in Italy, from north to south, she wrote, 'the sounds, the sights and the smells were indescribable. One would have to go back to Bethlem in 1815 to find parallels.' It is clear from what Professor Jones has written, and the 'lively correspondence' challenging her findings, that idealisation of the reforms in Italy, idealisation of *Gemeinshaft*, and the potential for translation of these fantasies to other jurisdictions, is still quite entrenched and resistant to reality testing.

Deinstitutionalisation began in the United States in the mid 1950s, following the development of chlorpromazine (largactil), and became part of the much larger 1960s War on Poverty programme implemented by the Kennedy-Johnson administration. The programme represents one of the biggest social experiments in American history. In 1955 there were 558,000 patients in state hospitals (population 164 million); in 1994 there were 72,000 (population 260 million). Given the proportions between inpatients and the national population in 1955 and 1994, the effective rate of deinstitutionalisation is in the region of 90%. Viewed another way, the USA has moved from a total of 339 occupied state beds per 100,000 of the population to 41 per 100,000. In California, there are only 14 state hospital beds per 100,000, including those for forensic patients. The impetus for the programme of bed closures has been driven by a combination of economics (the erroneous assertion that community care is cheaper than hospital care), ideology and civil rights.

Community care in the US has consistently failed to reach the most disadvantaged groups in its society: the ethnic minorities, the elderly, the poor and those living in decaying inner cities and scattered rural communities. Attempts have been made in some parts of the UK to introduce costly American-style assertive community treatment approaches, which have worked impressively in a few places like Madison, Wisconsin and elsewhere (*The Guardian*, 1998). On the whole, however, community care in the US is badly co-ordinated, under-resourced and dysfunctional. It fails to reach the people who need it most, particularly those who are resistant to treatment and/or who suffer from substance abuse.

In his recent book, *Out of the Shadows*, E. Fuller Torrey (1997) writes:

> 'Thus deinstitutionalisation has helped create the mental illness crisis by discharging people from public psychiatric hospitals without ensuring that they received the medication and rehabilitation services necessary for them to live successfully in the community. Deinstitutionalisation further exacerbated the situation because, once the public psychiatric beds had been closed, they were not available for people who later became mentally ill, and this situation continues up to the present. Consequently, approximately 2.2 million severely mentally ill people do not receive any psychiatric treatment.
>
> 'Deinstitutionalisation was based on the principle that severe mental illness should be treated in the least restrictive setting, in order to maintain the greatest degree of freedom, self-determination,

autonomy, dignity and integrity of body, mind and spirit for the individual while he or she participates in treatment or receives services. For a substantial minority, however, deinstitutionalisation has been a psychiatric Titanic. Their lives are virtually devoid of dignity or integrity of body, mind or spirit. Self-determination often means merely a choice of soup kitchens. The least restrictive setting frequently turns out to be a cardboard box, a prison cell, or a terror-filled existence plagued by both real and imaginary enemies.'

In the UK, in 1961, the late Enoch Powell, as Minister of Health, made his famous 'water towers' speech and proposed to close all the old asylums and cut the total number of psychiatric beds in half. This strategy was very much in line with his determination to cut public spending on the National Health Service, and had nothing to do a more enlightened, humanitarian approach to the care and treatment of the mentally ill, although the Government of the day had some powerful ideological rhetoric to hide behind if it needed it.

Powell expected the old institutions to be closed by the mid 1970s but progress was slow. The Government's (1989) white paper, '*Caring for People : Community Care in the Next Decade and Beyond*', itself a response to the 1988 Griffiths Report, emphasised the new drug treatments available for the treatment of mental illness, rendering 'the traditional large and often remote mental hospital' redundant. The white paper went on to affirm that 'the number of hospital beds should be reduced only as a consequence of the development of new services. Ministers will not approve the closure of any mental hospital unless it can be demonstrated that adequate alternatives have been developed.'

Community care : *Gesellschaft*

The past 15 years or so have seen an acceleration of the programme set out in the 1960s and developed during the 1970s. Unfortunately the motivation for this acceleration has been financial, not clinical. With so much of the funding tied up in inpatient care, it is natural for managers in the new NHS marketplace to want to release those funds as quickly as possible. With the closure of sites, one would expect significant funds to be made available for patient care in the community, but this has not happened. Lowin et al. (1998) go some way toward explaining why. Planning permission for a long stay hospital is 'institutional' use. Getting permission for 'residential' use is a lengthy and sometimes impossible process although, if successful, makes a marked difference on price per acre (£50,000 per acre to £250,000 per acre is one example mentioned). Although there were many commercial plans to develop them, many of the old sites remain vacant, long after the hospitals on them were closed.

Furthermore, each vacant site incurs maintenance costs and the consequent opportunity costs are even more substantial. The money that has been raised from site sales was meant to be ring-fenced, according to the Department of Health, but this has not happened either.

Community care has, therefore, been scandalously short-changed and we have witnessed the consequences of this throughout the 1990s. In spite of the introduction of the care programme approach, new guidance from the Department of Health, and a number of measures issuing out of Virginia Bottomley's Ten Point Plan, including new legislation introducing supervised discharge orders, and a number of highly critical reports and surveys about the state of mental health services, and even a new name for the policy from Stephen Dorrell ('The Spectrum of Care', February 1996), nothing has prevented the decline in services that we are now in danger of being asked to take for granted. This is a decline that has allowed morale and staffing in psychiatry to plummet (Deahl & Turner, 1997), forcing the Royal College of Psychiatrists (1997) to warn of the imminent 'collapse' of services, and (Thornicroft, 1998) of services that are 'half-hearted, half-minded and half-funded.' Nor is the prison service immune from the build-up of pressure (Needham-Bennett & Cumming, 1995)

There has evidently been a good deal of commentary, much of it well-informed and sophisticated, some of it highly technical, on what has gone wrong and how it can be put right. Tyrer (1998) says we are faced with two models of community care:

'a profligate model which is expensive, increases bed use and separates professionals, and a cost-effective one which is much cheaper, reduces bed use and promotes team work. The right choice is obvious and any observer taking a historical perspective of psychiatry in the last years of the 20th century would find it hard to explain why we have been so misled.'

Professor Tyrer feels confident that lessons have been learned and that community care can be put back on course again. Many of the lessons learned have come from the terrible human tragedies recorded in the independent inquiries into homicides committed by mentally ill people.

The independent inquiries

In 1996 The Zito Trust published the second edition of *Learning The Lessons* (Sheppard, 1996) which summarises the independent inquiries and sets out their recommendations under a number of separate practice headings, including those recommendations made by the inquiry reports which are directed at central government. We have always felt that *Learning The Lessons* contains enough experience to implement community care throughout the entire world, let alone in the UK. Indeed, the Clunis inquiry said more than enough about what is wrong and how it should be put right.

At February 1998, according to a written answer in the House of Commons, there have been 32 published homicide inquiry reports set up under Hèalth Service Guidelines issued in 1994 (HSG(94)27); that is, since the publication of the Clunis report. A list of these is published in the Appendix. There are, apparently, a further 24 inquiries under way. Other homicides have yet to reach court which may require this type of inquiry.

Guidelines on the management of independent inquiries are contained in the NHS Executive's 'Guidance on the discharge of mentally disordered people and their continuing care in the community' (HSG(94)27). Under the sub-section 'If Things Go Wrong', the procedure that needs to be followed is set out accordingly:

'33. If a violent incident occurs, it is important not only to respond to the immediate needs of the patient and others involved, but in serious cases also to learn lessons for the future...

'34. Additionally, after the completion of any legal proceedings it may be necesssary to hold an independent inquiry. *In cases of homicide, it will always be necessary to hold an inquiry which is independent of the providers involved.*' (NHS italics)

This guidance was re-visited in 1996 in *Building Bridges*, part of the Government's Health of the Nation Strategy. In Chapter 5 of *Building Bridges*, 'If Things Go Wrong', the following sub-section is headed 'External inquiries':

'5.1.17 If an incident is sufficiently serious, it is inappropriate to rely solely on an internal investigation. It will not always be immediately obvious whether an incident is 'serious' enough to warrant an external investigation. However, any incident, or series of incidents, which appear to call into question existing procedures, may warrant a more formal investigation.'

It is becoming increasingly clear that this guidance is not being strictly adhered to, even in the case of homicide. Following the death of 57 year old Carla Thompson in Tulse Hill in January 1998, an announcement was quickly made by South Thames NHS Executive Regional Office that, given what was known about the circumstances of the death, it had ordered an independent inquiry into services provided by three separate NHS trusts and one local authority social services department (Bethlem & Maudsley, Lambeth Healthcare, Pathfinder Mental Health Services, and Lambeth Social Services). It has since become apparent, however, (*Health Service Journal*, 1998) that this is going to be an internal inquiry with an independent chair, which is not quite the same thing and marks a significant departure from NHS guidance.

In cases of serious violence which does not lead to death, the situation is just as worrying, as the following case being handled by The Zito Trust graphically illustrates:

Hugh Coll

On 18 February 1997, Hugh Coll, aged 50, was returning home from his night shift as a tunneller working for Tarmac on the Jubilee Line Extension Project. At 5am at a bus stop on the Seven Sisters Road he was viciously stabbed by a complete stranger, subsequently identified as Joel Roberts, a former patient at Friern Barnet Hospital, now closed. Hugh Coll lost most of his body's blood and 'died' three times on the operating table. The surgeon said he had never seen such horrific injuries and had to take time off to recover. Joel Roberts gave himself up at Wood Green police station, saying he dreamed he had stabbed someone. At the Old Bailey in November 1997 Roberts, who pleaded not guilty to any charges, was found guilty of attempted murder and was detained in a secure unit under sections 37/41 of the Mental Health Act 1983. The trial judge, the Recorder of London, Sir Lawrence Verney, observed that the failure of those who should have been caring for Roberts 'had terrible consequences' but, it appeared, no one was admitting blame. He went on to say that 'this is yet another example of the concept of care in the community going woefully wrong. He slipped through the net of the services this country has to offer.'

Hugh Coll will never work again. He is permananently scarred, physically and psychologically. He and his wife Madge have a family of six children, five of whom live at home and are dependent. As a tunneller, Hugh would have been earning between £30-40,000 a year. After the attack he received a letter from his employers, Tarmac, dated 30 May 1997 which said, 'As you are unable to perform the tasks for which you were employed, it is with deep regret that we give you one week's notice of redundancy commencing on 6 June 1997. You...will receive one week's full pay for this notice period.'

In February 1998, Hugh Coll's application for legal aid to pursue the health authority responsible for the care and treatment of Joel Roberts was turned down, following the court of appeal decision in the Clunis case in December 1997. The Zito Trust has been advised by North Thames NHS Executive Regional Office that an internal inquiry into Roberts' care has been carried out by Haringey Health Care Trust. No one is allowed to read this report. As far as the family is concerned, such an inquiry is of no value to them. Their MP is fully involved. They think of taking the case to Europe. Frustrated with the formal procedures, the family turned to the media and the story was carried by a number of newspapers, BBC1 and national radio. *The Daily Mail* published its report of the case on 17 November 1997, having carried out some inquiries of its own:

> 'The court heard he had served with distinction in the Royal Green Jackets before sustaining a leg injury in Northern Ireland. He had suffered from schizophrenia for ten years and had been treated in various hospitals. On his release, however, he failed to take his medication and went unchecked by social services.
>
> 'The Daily Mail has found that Roberts had spent time at Friern Barnet Hospital in North London, was treated by a psychiatrist at St Ann's Hospital in Finsbury Park and had also been an out-patient at North Middlesex Hospital.
>
> 'In 1990 he was jailed for 42 days for two assaults and carrying a weapon. He had rowed with a fellow passenger on a train and produced a knife. In 1995 he received a conditional discharge after losing his temper in a traffic dispute and driving into a police officer.
>
> 'Neighbours had become increasingly concerned about the behaviour of the keen boxer, who believed his housing association flat in Wood Green was bugged. They said he was excessively houseproud but had an odd habit of 'planting' poems and phrases in pots and kept a bath full of dead goldfish.'

His estranged wife is reported by the newspaper as saying, 'I know he wouldn't have taken medication because that would be an admission that he was ill.'

The case of Hugh Coll is set out in full for a number of reasons, not least its uncomfortable resemblance to the death of Jonathan Zito in the same part of north London over four years previously. So it is alleged that Joel Roberts kept dead goldfish in the bath, which is surely his right? But in the wider context, should anyone have expressed more than just passing concern about this odd behaviour? One is reminded of Christopher Clunis returning burned books to Wood Green library, which no one thought to question or follow up. There are also, allegedly, the previous contacts with criminal justice and health professionals by Roberts which do not seem to have been considered all that serious at the time, again reminding us of the 'catalogue of missed opportunities' reported by the Clunis inquiry. Only, in the Coll case we shall probably never know the truth about how similar these cases really are, which only an independent inquiry will reveal. So we are all left speculating, including the media.

On the subject of independent inquiries, a number of commentaries, views and opinions about the future management of them have been published or expressed in recent times. It is well known that the Department of Health has been looking at this issue and has sought the views of a number of different individuals and organisations, including The Zito Trust.

Perhaps the clearest expression of the two sides of the argument is set out in two opposing editorials in *Psychiatric Bulletin* by Muijen (1997) and Grounds (1997).

Muijen states that the 'barrage of inquiry reports....has served few people well'. His view is that they are costly, they add little that has not already been stated and that they lead to defensive practices on the part of the professionals involved in mental health delivery, and that the public is fed misleading impressions of the danger posed by the mentally ill living in the community. It is interesting to note Muijen's concern for the victims and their relatives, that inquiries constantly remind them of 'the tragedy that has befallen them' and they therefore 'find it hard to get on with their lives'. While he is not opposed to accountability, his proposal is for a system whereby an authoritative individual or body sifts through 'incident reports' and decides what level of audit or inquiry is necessary in each case. Panel inquiries, presumably he means *independent* panel inquiries, would only be ordered in exceptional cases, 'where due to their novelty [sic] or public concern such an inquiry seems necessary.' Suggestions for the kind of body which could oversee such a process include the National Confidential Inquiry, the Health Advisory Service, the Social Services Inspectorate and the Mental Health Act Commission.

In his response to Muijen, Grounds agrees that some central coordination of the present arrangements is required, a view endorsed by The Zito Trust. He goes on to say that independent inquiries continue to be needed, and his arguments may be summarised as follows:

- The public interest demands that inquiries into this category of homicide are public, not private.

- Independent inquiries are of crucial importance to families who have been bereaved, so that they have the opportunity of finding out from an objective source what really happened, and that what happened to them does not happen to others.

- Inquiries are a means of public education. They draw attention to good and bad practice and convey a better understanding of the limitations of mental health services.

- Inquiries raise the profile of mental health issues and provide pressure for much needed resources.

- Issues of local importance, when publicised, have general application.

- Psychiatric scandals are important levers for longer-term reform.

It is difficult to see how public accountability can be maintained in this area without the current degree of independence. In an otherwise critical review of mental health services throughout the country, the Royal College of Psychiatrists (1997) question the current inquiry system for being inordinately expensive and damaging to public confidence and staff morale, while accepting the need for public accountability. In the College's view, this can be achieved through the 'mechanisms of legal proceedings, disciplinary proceedings, inquests and the National Confidential Inquiry into Homicides and Suicides by Mentally Ill People', without the additional need of a 'further costly health authority panel'.

How these proposed mechanisms would achieve the desired result - public accountability - is not clear. Criminal proceedings do not investigate the circumstances leading to the homicide or untoward attack in any depth. Some defendants are found unfit to plead, others commit suicide. In many cases of homicide by mentally ill people, the result is manslaughter on the grounds of diminished responsibility, meaning there is no need for a full examination of the facts. The criminal court, therefore, is not a reliable forum for finding out what went wrong. Judges often make the point that a full inquiry is recommended but that it is not up to them to carry one out. Civil legal proceedings in this field have signally failed, so far, to get under way. Christopher Clunis' claim for damages for breach of duty of care against Camden & Islington Health Authority was thrown out by the court of appeal on the grounds, firstly, that it was not in the public interest that someone in his position, having committed a crime, should seek to benefit financially and, secondly, no common law duty of care arises from s.117 of the Mental Health Act 1983.

This has been followed more recently by the High Court in another case arising out of the Shaun Armstrong inquiry. These decisions have clearly influenced the Legal Aid Board in their refusal to grant legal aid to Hugh Coll and his family.

Disciplinary proceedings are rare in this field. One of the conclusions to be drawn from all of the published inquiry reports is that disciplinary proceedings are not expected and do not have a part to play in the process of apportioning blame to individuals or in making them accountable for mistakes they made.

Inquests, also listed by the Royal College of Psychiatrists, somewhat strangely, as a possible alternative investigative process to independent inquiries, are not trials and do not attempt to establish responsibility or liability. Inquests are established to find out the identity of the person who has died and the cause and circumstances of the death. They do not have the authority or the means to undertake prolonged and detailed inquiries into psychiatric histories and the precise circumstances which led to the tragedy.

The reality we are left with is stark. If the mechanism set out in HSG(94)27 and *Building Bridges* is allowed to become more and more diluted, or open to interpretation, or just simply ignored, we will be left with a community care policy which has no checks or balances, no procedures for learning lessons from 'mistakes', and no system of accountability. One day, perhaps, even the media will lose interest and people like Jonathan Zito and Hugh Coll will be stabbed as they wait for public transport, and the whys and the wherefores will be completely ignored.

Stigma

One of the criticisms frequently levelled at commentators on mental health issues, especially when the focus of the commentary is on some of the potentially more contentious areas (homicide, violence, non-compliance etc), is that publicity about these matters reinforces the general public's perceptions about the mentally ill, and makes it more difficult for them to be accepted by the community. Organisations representing the interests of users, in partcular, are quick to under-estimate the scale of the problems being addressed by the media and say that enormous damage is done to the interests of the mentally ill by people whose opinions are formed by lurid tabloid headlines. The attempts by local authorities and the voluntary sector to set up community homes in residential areas are thwarted by what is seen as unnecessary scaremongering and hostility leading, in some cases, to the abandonment of these development plans, to the detriment of the patients and of community care policy.

It is certainly true that the lay media is very interested in community care. It is also true that it is generally not very interested in examples of community care which work effectively and well. A perceived excessive interest by the media on the dramatic consequences of community care breakdown has led, for example, to the development of Mediawatch by a number of mental health charities, to a new set of standards about media reporting on mental health issues by the Broadcasting Standards Commission, and to various initiatives by the mental health industry to combat alleged discrimination of the mentally ill in the crucial areas of employment, housing, education and leisure.

Undoubtedly there are several related issues here. The key task is to recognise where the problems lie in the development and implementation of community care policy, to learn from experience, and to have a serious debate about what has gone wrong and what changes might make a difference, however uncomfortable such a debate might be. It would, no doubt, be preferable on some level, and for some people, if we were to ignore the problems and not discuss them in public in the hope that, eventually, they will go away.

To take one example, there has for some time been a vague assumption, about homicide statistics, that the number of homicides committed by mentally ill people has not gone up, or that it has gone down, or that it has remained the same - for the past ten, twenty, thirty or even forty years. This assumption was re-stated as recently as March 1998 (*The Guardian*, 1998). Yet as The Zito Trust has pointed out in correspondence and articles in the specialist and general press, it is not possible to make such an assumption about homicides by the mentally ill based on statistics currently collated annually by the Home Office. This much has been agreed by the Home Office (personal communication), so why is this confusing and imprecise mantra still given an outing every time there is a discussion of any kind about community care? There is more on this particular issue in Chapter 6 of this report, where we look in detail at what the statistics do tell us.

Then there is the important assumption that debate about these issues really does stigmatise the mentally ill. The assumption is based on the perceived effects of media sensationalisation of homicides and violent attacks by mentally ill people in the community. Inherent in this assumption, of course, is a somewhat patronising view of the general public as crude, unintelligent, uninformed and unable to defend themselves against banner tabloid headlines describing a frenzied stabbing by a patient recently discharged from a psychiatric hospital.

The assumption that the media, in all its forms, is that influential in people's lives has recently come under increasing scrutiny, particularly concerning the impact of violence in films, and the influence of various types of cartoon violence on young children. This is not the place to widen such a complex discussion. In the field of mental health, however, it is possible to question the myth about the stigmatisation of the mental illness by the public in response to what they read and hear.

In September 1997 MORI conducted a poll commissioned by Fleishman Hillard UK, using a panel of healthcare professionals and the National Schizophrenia Fellowship to advise on the questions for the survey. The main objectives of the research were to find out among the general public:

- the level of awareness of attitudes towards schizophrenia
- attitudes towards services which might help someone with schizophrenia live in the community
- the level of tolerance towards people with schizophrenia

A nationally representative sample of 1,804 adults aged 15 plus was interviewed across 167 constituency-based sampling points. Among the findings were the following, relevant to this discussion:

- 72% said that with careful support and appropriate treatment with modern medicines, people with schizophrenia can live successfully in the community.

- 73% said the provision of a long-term care plan was essential to help a person suffering from schizophrenia live in the community. 58% felt it was important for society to understand the illness.

- 39% saw medication as the most important way in which health and social services could help someone suffering from schizophrenia live in the local community. 34% felt supportive local counselling was the most important factor, with 33% stressing the provision of information for carers.

- Only 12% said that people with schizophrenia should live in institutions for the mentally ill.

- Only 18% said they would not be willing to work alongside someone with schizophrenia.

In its conclusions, the MORI report states that 'recognition of schizophrenia as a form of mental illness is high' and that 'that the public gives roughly equal weight to professional support and to support from the family to enable people with schizophrenia to lead a normal life. Friends and support groups come in at a close second..' The need for close support and local counselling, as well as medication, is emphasised, in addition to 'the overwhelming response...for a long-term care plan.' The public, the survey shows, 'is also aware of the need to inform and educate society generally about schizophrenia.' Finally, 'It is encouraging to find that as many as 72% feel that with careful support and appropriate treatment with modern medicines, people with schizophrenia can live successfully in the community.'

Indeed it is. What is also fascinating about this survey is that it updates a similar poll carried out by MORI in 1990, and shows how public attitudes towards schizophrenia as an illness, and towards the community as the best option for people suffering from schizophrenia, have improved over a period of time in which there have been a large number of high profile homicides, suicides and untoward attacks and incidents. This is period of seven years or so, during which there has been unprecedented interest and concern by the media, by central government, at numerous conferences and from the national and specialist publishing industries. This is a time when mental health and community care has risen from its lowly place on the floor of social policy and has moved swiftly up the public agenda, occupying a space it has never been in before. It is clear the public has, on the whole, listened carefully to the debate. It has certainly become more aware of the issues, and more sensitive in its response to them, and appears to have sound ideas about where the mentally ill should be cared for, by whom and with what kind of support in place. A pity, then, that we did not ask them before because in their response to the questions put, the much-maligned general public appears to have come up with some of right answers.

Finally

This report is being published at a time when the future development of community care policy is at a crossroads. There is a new Government in office which has expressed its concern and its determination to address the fundamental issues (*The Daily Telegraph*, 1998). A new Independent Reference Group has been established by the NHS Executive to advise the Minister on mental health matters, but which has already come in for criticism (*The Times*, 1998) for being 'hastily composed' and for not having among its membership 'a single full-time practising psychiatrist.' There is, however, consensus that reform is needed, but not much consensus about the content and direction of reform. Some difficult issues will need to be debated over the next two to three years. A draft policy document leaked from within the NHS in February 1997 set out an action plan for reform which might or might not see a new Mental Health Act on the statute books by 2001. Clearly there now exists a real opportunity to create a broad spectrum of mental health services, underpinned by legislation that is both therapeutic and robust which will provide for the needs of patients, professionals and the public, from high security care to care in the community.

This report sets out which areas, in our view, need to be considered seriously when reforms are being debated over the next two to three years. One thing we are certain of: reform must be based on hard evidence and not on fantasy.

Although I am responsible for the contents of this report, I am grateful to a number of individuals for their help in producing it. They include: Jayne Zito (Patron, The Zito Trust), Peter Hill, Corrine Charles, Andrew Lloyd, Dr Vivien Norris and Dave Sheppard (Director, Institute of Mental Health Law).

Michael Howlett
The Zito Trust, London
April 1998

References

Deahl, M. and Turner, T. (1997) 'General psychiatry in no-man's land'. *British Journal of Psychiatry*, 171: 6-8.

Grounds, A. (1997) Commentary on "Inquiries: Who needs them?". *Psychiatric Bulletin*, 21: 134-5.

Health Service Journal (1998) Trust inquiry into attack on two women. 29 January.

Jones, K. and Poletti, A. (1986) 'The 'Italian Experience' Reconsidered'. *British Journal of Psychiatry*, 148: 144-50.

Lowin, A., Knapp, M. and Beecham J. (1998) 'Uses of old long-stay hospital buildings'. *Psychiatric Bulletin*, 22: 129-30.

Muijen, M. (1997) Inquiries: Who needs them? *Psychiatric Bulletin*, 21: 132-3.

Needham-Bennett, H. and Cumming, I. (1995) 'Waiting for a disaster to happen'. *British Medical Journal*, 311: 516-17.

Robertson, J.A. (1994) 'Community psychiatry: weasel words?' *Psychiatric Bulletin*, 18: 760-1.

Royal College of Psychiatrists (1997) *A Manifesto for Mental Health: Rebuilding Mental Health Services For the 21st Century*. London: Royal College of Psychiatrists.

Sheppard, D. (1996) *Learning The Lessons: Mental Health Inquiry Reports Published in England and Wales between 1969 and 1996 and their Recommendations for Improving Practice*. 2nd Edition. London: Zito Trust.

The Daily Telegraph (1998) Care in the community is scrapped. 17 January.

The Guardian (1998) Assertive outreach hope over care in the community 9 March.

Thornicroft, G. (1998) 'Doing it by halves'. *The Guardian*, 11 February.

Torrey, E.F. (1997) *Out of the Shadows: confronting America's mental illness crisis*. New York: Wiley.

Tyrer, P. (1998)'Cost-effective or profligate community psychiatry?' *British Journal of Psychiatry*, 172:1-3

Weller, M. (1998) Community care of the mentally ill (letter). *The Times*, 24 February.

CHAPTER ONE

THE INDEPENDENT INQUIRIES
PURCHASERS AND PROVIDERS

Introduction

Before analysing the independent homicide inquiries in which non-compliance with medication played a significant part in the circumstances leading to the homicide, we felt it would be beneficial to seek the views of some of those commissioning agencies where there had been inquiries on a range of issues arising from them. Accordingly, Jayne Zito, Patron of The Zito Trust, had a series of meetings towards the end of 1997, with senior management at the following commissioning authorities:

North West London Mental Health (NHS) Trust	(Boland, Buchanan inquiries)
Kensington & Chelsea and Westminster Health Authority	(Boland inquiry)
Tees Health Authority	(Taylor, Armstrong inquiries)
Leicestershire Health Authority	(Burton inquiry)
Redbridge and Waltham Forest Health Authority	(Mabota, Hampshire inquiries)

In total, seven independent inquiries were covered. Letters from The Zito Trust requesting meetings stated our purpose as being to discuss the particular inquiries in some depth and to ascertain how the commissioning authorities had responded to them, and to seek their views on a range of matters concerning the management and experience of independent inquiries and on the future development of mental health policy. Full notes of each meeting were sent back to the authorities concerned for approval, and these were then collated and analysed in such a way as to ensure that the full range of views was recorded as an overview while maintaining respect for confidentiality as to the provenance of individual views. This degree of confidentiality was agreed beforehand so that views could be given with greater freedom and frankness. The overview is summarised and the term 'authority' is used to include all those agencies visited.

Independent inquiries

Concerns were raised by nearly all the authorities visited about the quality of some of the investigations that take place during the inquiry process. Staff often feel they have been criticised on the basis of evidence that is distorted or incomplete, leading to questionable conclusions. There was a feeling that inquiry panels arrived at their own conclusions before assimilating all of the evidence, occasionally leading to the finding that some homicides were preventable, even predictable, when the complete evidence suggests they were not. The impact of the inquiries has been mixed, some authorities reporting benefits and lessons that can be learned, including important information and understanding for bereaved families and relatives, while other consequences are seen as less helpful, especially the financial cost and the damage to staff morale. There was a strong feeling that authorities had been 'dumped' with an expensive and potentially draining inquiry process in a wider context of poor leadership in mental health from central government.

One authority commented that the inquiries make a positive contribution to the activity of pushing mental health to the forefront of purchasing, breaking down barriers and pushing through the agenda, but went on to comment that the time lapse between the homicide, the internal inquiry and the independent inquiry made it extremely difficult to implement effective measures for the improvement of services. The same authority expressed concern about potentially damaging publicity, leading to mistrust of existing services by users and carers.

More than one authority criticised the practice of appointing lawyers, more often than not barristers, to chair inquiries, as they tended to adopt a legalistic, over-formal approach which many staff found distressing. The view that an internal inquiry with an independent evaluator would be an adequate process was widely shared. All accepted the need for public accountability.

The management of difficult patients

Concerns about the authorities' responsibilities towards the management of difficult patients included the following:

1. At present there is no ownership of the chaotic and dangerous patients, and a much better understanding is needed of a small group of people for the wider benefit of patient and public.

2. Difficult patients who need medium to high level security are blocking acute beds and absorbing a disproportionate amount of the funding.

3. If difficult patients, who can have multiple needs, including substance abuse and/or personality disorder, do not meet the criteria for detention and will not voluntarily accept treatment, the only option is to 'wait until something happens' so that treatment can be given involuntarily.

4. Personality disordered patients are currently denied a service because they are deemed to be untreatable.

5. Difficult patients in the community require constant supervision.

6. It is necessary to accept that these patients will have to be placed somewhere, in 'someone's back yard'.

7. GPs have no experience or training in dealing with the severely mentally ill.

8. Many practitioners regard the skills needed to work with the severely mentally ill as 'backward nursing' and 'not attractive professionally'.

The care programme approach

All authorities confirmed that the care programme approach (cpa) had been implemented but expressed a number of problems with it. Included among these were the failure of new IT systems which meant that sophisticated monitoring was very difficult to achieve. Staff were reported as being resistant to working as members of multi-disciplinary teams, with keyworkers often failing to attend meetings on a regular basis. Some authorities stated that the cpa was there in quantity but not in quality, and that it brings with it an enormous workload which in itself absorbs precious resources. There is, in some respects, limited incentive to develop the cpa without extra resources linked to its enhanced implementation.

Noticeable was the emphasis placed on the need to convince practitioners, especially psychiatrists, that the cpa reflects good practice rather than a bureaucratic nightmare.

On a local basis, concern was expressed that the lack of high level, supported accommodation in the community made it difficult to implement good practice as far as the cpa was concerned, with up to 20-30 patients in hospital ready to be discharged and occupying beds which could either be used for other patients, or which could be closed, thereby releasing resources. When the cpa is working well, which is rarely, extra contractual referrals virtually drop to zero, but if just one local community mental health team is not working effectively the pressure on bed management is acute. One authority described a proposal to replace consultant led care with a GP fundholding model for mental health, a unique innovation which would see a GP appointed manager for mental health co-ordinating and leading the community mental health teams. This kind of innovation is seen as vital, with the clear recognition that GPs currently have little idea about what the cpa involves.

Most of the authorities questioned felt strongly that those consultants whose work is poor, and sometimes negligent, not only damaged the entire system of community mental health provision but were almost impossible to sack. Even when inquiries rightly criticised consultants, they remained in post, almost obdurately, and a lot of work had to go on 'behind the scenes' to force them to resign. One authority criticised the General Medical Council for its over-protection of consultants generally, with its defensive codes and strict guidance, which means consultants are rarely found guilty of malpractice.

Compulsory supervision or treatment

The new supervised discharge orders were viewed with some scepticism, although they were recognised as raising the awareness of staff about individual patients, and their needs, and the need to concentrate on individualised packages of care. But these aftercare packages have significant resource implications and the orders were introduced without the extra funding needed to implement them. There is widespread concern that these orders require a named keyworker who becomes legally responsible for the patient without giving them any extra powers, which is why they are not frequently used. Supervised discharge orders require the patient's agreement, without which it is impossible to get them to comply.

On the issue of compulsory treatment orders, the majority felt they should have been introduced in the new legislation (Mental Health (Patients in the Community) Act 1995), to support supervised discharge orders, and that an important opportunity to do so was missed. It was clear that for some patients, who should not be discharged into the community, only compulsory treatment orders will enable teams to work with them when they are discharged. This group includes difficult and challenging patients who often have transient lifestyles and a history of substance abuse in addition to severe mental illness. It was felt that the civil liberties of the patient could be protected by checks and monitors included in new legislation, including the right of appeal to mental health review tribunals and/or the Mental Health Act Commission. It was also pointed out that the current Mental Health Act 1983 is rarely used as it could be (eg guardianship, health and welfare criteria for compulsory admission).

One authority felt it was incumbent upon the professional role of the mental health worker to ensure that the patient was compliant with treatment, placing more of an emphasis on good keyworker/patient relationships, rather than coercive legislation. It was recognised that this approach was dependent for its success on good working practices and good staff morale, well supported by management. The same authority felt strongly that the new anti-psychotic drug treatments, with their much improved side-effect profile, would help in such an approach, and that it was 'scandalous' that conventional compounds were still being prescribed on the grounds of cost or ignorance. It was also felt that guidance on supervised discharge orders could be tightened up, obviating the need for further new legislation.

In general the view was that non-compliant patients were made more difficult to work with because mental health professionals were not allowed to intervene more pro-actively or assertively with them, even when they could see problems stacking up, and more often than not, left them alone. One respondent said 'it is ridiculous that staff are required to negotiate with potential killers.'

Other issues

Resources: patients are staying in secure units for longer periods of time due to a shortage of alternative services. Since the introduction of standardised risk assessment protocols, one authority complained that its extra contractual referral bill had shot up by £2.5m. The shortage of locally based alternative inpatient facilities, particularly new long-stay, was a theme common to all of the respondents.

Central Government: various points were directed at central government for urgent consideration, in addition to issues raised already in this chapter:

1. A need to improve training in psychiatry and nursing to reflect the needs of patients predominantly being cared for in the community. One authority described current ('dinosaur') training methods as unable to distinguish outpatient from inpatient care.

2. A need to resource a primary care led service, following a national review of policy with clear direction on the funding of community care and how inter-agency collaboration is to be achieved.

3. A need for nationally developed, standardised risk assessment tools, to be implemented nationally.

4. A more effective strategy to improve the interface between the criminal justice system and the NHS. The pressure to take high security patients from the special hospitals, with their longer-term needs, places significant pressure on an already over-stretched system, and must be properly funded.

5. The need to train GPs in mental health care delivery and to get them to recognise and accept their part in community mental health teams. 'Get them to read the Mental Health Act', as one respondent put it.

6. A need to clarify and define treatability criteria for psychopathic and personality disordered patients. One authority said 'The current situation is crazy and reflects its own madness. The general public find it inconceivable that at present we discharge highly dangerous patients into our communities because they are deemed untreatable by the system'.

7. Policy from the centre needs to be driven and resourced by a better understanding about how the hospital closure programme over the past 15 years has taken place in a context of increasing social problems which have not been adequately recognised and incorporated into official policy development. This includes higher crime rates, especially crimes of

violence, lack of housing, homelessness, unemployment, alcohol and substance abuse, all of which place great pressure on mental health services.

8. Review the issue of patient confidentiality with the General Medical Council.

The Zito Trust would like to place on record its gratitude to the authorities involved in these meetings, and especially to those individuals who gave up their time to discuss these issues. The meetings were, without exception, open and constructive.

CHAPTER TWO

TREATMENT IN THE COMMUNITY WITHOUT CONSENT

Introduction

Few areas of mental health policy give rise to more anxiety and debate than treatment in the community without consent. Variously described and proposed as community treatment orders or community supervision orders, the prospect of treatment without consent becoming an integral part of community care policy as we enter the new millenium will no doubt focus the minds of both sides of the divide as they engage in the lobbying, debating and consulting to come and which might, or might not, lead to reform.

Is reform needed? Are the powers required to 'bind in' patients to community services already in place? Should the state be commissioned to extend its powers, or create new powers, thereby further eroding individual civil liberties? Is the proposal for greater increased legislative muscle in this area of policy no more than a desire to forge a new and bigger sledgehammer to crack what many perceive to be a relatively small problem?

This chapter does not seek to explore the entire history of compulsory treatment. Comprehensive accounts can be found in many contemporary histories of psychiatry. Perhaps the best on the market is Fennell (1996), and much of what follows owes a debt to this work in particular, and to a paper reviewing proposals for compulsory supervision by Exworthy (1995). What follows is no more than a modest attempt to widen the context in which some of these issues are set.

The Mental Health (Patients in the Community) Act 1995 ('the 1995 Act') introduced a new power of supervised discharge directed at detained patients who, it was felt, posed a risk to themselves or others, and who would benefit from greater powers of supervision on discharge from hospital. The new powers are not widely used. In a study carried out by the Care Programme Approach Association, and published in April 1997 in its journal *The Approach*, it was discovered that in the 52 areas looked at, covering a total population of over 15 million people, only 32 patients were subject to supervised discharge orders, compared to 1000 on supervision registers and nearly 4000 entitled to aftercare services under s.117 of the Mental Health Act 1983. There are wide geographical variations in the use of these powers and a good deal of scepticism and criticism about them from clinicians and community mental health teams.

The 1995 Act applies to Scotland, where it has served to cut the former widespread and unlimited use of extended leave of absence to just 12 months. Until 1996, when the 1995 Act came into force, 'compulsory treatment' was used in Scotland via the means of leave of absence of unrestricted duration. Dyer (1998) reports that at the end of 1994 there were 129 people who had been on leave of absence for over 12 months, 17 of them for over three years and five for over four years. The most common reason cited for extended leave of absence was the assessment made of patients that they were likely to stop taking their medication. With leave of absence extended to beyond 12 months, patients could be recalled to hospital and treatment given. One of the consequences of the 1995 Act in Scotland, revealed in the 1996-97 Annual Report of the Mental Welfare Commission for Scotland, is that there are only 20 patients on community care orders (the equivalent to supervised discharge orders under the 1995 Act). This, the report concludes, echoes the Commission's previous concerns that these new orders will not be used by psychiatrists 'because they do not contain a clear means of ensuring that patients in the absence of their consent continue to take medication.'

The 1995 Act was implemented, in part, as a response to the perceived failure to use the guardianship powers which have been available since the Mental Health Act 1959. Originally directed at health authorities, guardianship subsequently became the responsibility of local authorities before returning to health authorities in the form of supervised discharge orders under the 1995 Act. The requirements made of patients under supervision are very similar to those under guardianship and the 1995 Act, but neither are used consistently enough to have widespread impact. There is no doubt that guardianship can be effective (Blom-Cooper et al, 1995).

In the case of guardianship, psychiatrists used a short cut to circumvent the bureaucratic form-filling, application process (a current criticism of supervised discharge orders) by using their powers to grant leave which was conditional on compliance with medication in the community. As this procedure was not legal, patients would have to go back to hospital for a night to have the period of 'detention' renewed so they could go back out on conditional leave. This creative use of extended leave came to end following the judicial outcome of two leading cases in 1986, *Hallstrom* and *Gardner*, where it was made clear that treatment could not be given without consent unless there was clear statutory authority to support it.

This led to a flurry of activity from the Royal College of Psychiatrists (1987), culminating in the College's proposal for the introduction of community supervision orders (Royal College of Psychiatrists, 1993) and rejection of them by the Health Committee of the House of Commons (1993). It would be helpful, in terms of setting out some of the arguments on both sides, if we consider the College's proposal, and the subsequent Health Committee's response, in more detail.

Community supervision orders

The Royal College of Psychiatrists (1993) described its proposal for community supervision orders (cso) as a measure to deal directly with 'revolving door patients.' The cso would sanction the compulsory supervision of patients in the community who had previously been compulsorily detained in hospital. It was felt to be the most efficacious means of intervening in order to prevent deterioration to the extent that a further admission to hospital would become necessary

The cso would only be implemented where patients had been previously sectioned under sections 3 or 37 of the Mental Health Act 1983. Patients must give prior consent to a cso for compulsory supervision of their treatment in the community, they must have a history of relapse leading to readmission as a result of a refusal to comply with treatment in the community and the refusal to comply must have led to a deterioration in their condition. The order can be renewed after six months, and then again after another six months, and then annually for up to at least three years. Application for a cso is made by the responsible medical officer (rmo) and one other registered general practitioner, supported by a report from an approved social worker.

The effect of the order is enable the rmo, supported by another doctor appointed by the Mental Health Act Commission, to recall a patient to hospital for treatment if, having previously agreed to a cso, the patient fails to comply with any aspect of the order. The status of a recalled patient would be that of a patient detained under section 3 of the 1983 Act. The patient would, therefore, have the right to apply to a mental health review tribunal to be discharged from the order.

It was clear that the College's proposal was designed to apply to a small number of patients who failed consistently to take medication in the community.

The College was unclear about the numbers of patients that would be affected by the cso. It was thought to be a very small but 'difficult group to manage'. The cso should allow psychiatrists to manage them better in the community for longer periods than would otherwise be possible.

The Health Committee of the House of Commons

In examining the College's proposal for the introduction of compulsory supervision orders the Committee explored a number of issues, beginning with an examination of which type of patients, and how many, would be effected. A number of estimates by witnesses to the Committee were made, and these estimates ranged from 2500 to 4000, although the College's criteria for including or defining patient categories were not considered to be very clear.

The Committee examined existing powers to detain patients under sections 2, 3 and 4 of the 1983 Act. It heard evidence that suggested clinicians did not adequately understand their full powers under the existing legislation; in particular, it was clear that a significant number of psychiatrists only admitted patients to hospital on the grounds of safety, after their condition had deteriorated to a considerable degree, although the 1983 Act and the 1993 Code of Practice permit detention in the interests of the patient's own health. The committee also heard evidence concerning the under use of guardianship powers and how some alterations to existing powers of guardianship could render them more effective and more widely used. These 'improvements' became enshrined in the 1995 Act.

The Committee listened to evidence from organisations representing users which suggested that patients receiving treatment in the community under care management and the care programme approach fared significantly better than those who were coerced into treatment by more traditionally legalistic procedures. These groups proposed options which would not require further legislative change, emphasising the need for psychiatrists to have a better understanding of existing powers. A great deal of optimism and hope was placed on the care programme approach which, at the time, was by no means fully implemented. They did not feel that the College's community supervision orders were either necessary or desirable. It was felt that introducing them would create considerable overlap with the cpa and care management

Further emphasis was placed on the need for more resources to provide respite and crisis intervention care as a more desirable method of treating the severely mentally ill, thereby effectively avoiding hospital admission in the event of a deterioration in a patient's condition.

The Committee heard evidence that better information provided about the side- effects and long-term effects of medication would allow patients to make informed decisions about compliance with prescribed treatments. Further emphasis was placed on the need to improve relationships between patient and professional if long-term care planning was to be implemented and delivered successfully. It was felt that the cso proposal ignored the fundamental reasons for non-compliance and that its implementation would undermine this essential relationship between patient and professional, leading to further mistrust and paranoia about the inherent threat of hospitalisation. The special concerns of the homeless mentally ill, along with ethnic minorities, were considered to have been ignored by the proposal. Evidence was heard which suggested that the cso would contravene the European Convention on human rights.

The Committee concluded that the College's proposal was 'unworkable' and 'flawed' and was unable to recommend it to Parliament. The significant factor in its determination was the issue of consent. The code of practice to the 1983 Act places a number of conditions or tests to ensure that a patient is able to provide informed and demonstrable consent to medical treatment. This test of consent is applicable to patients who have been compulsorily detained. The Committee concluded that a cso must meet this test in advance and it was unclear from the proposal how a patient could withdraw consent when such a withdrawal could then introduce the element of compulsion into treatment. The Committee felt that the proposal invited the patient to 'sign away their right to refuse medication or other treatment'. For the Committee, the necessary balance between statutory powers and their encroachment on individual civil liberties had not been struck, although it recognised that such powers would be effective in many instances in making patients compliant with medication who would otherwise remain non-compliant. Additional statutory powers would require consensus between both users and carers and, in the Committee's view, this consensus had not been achieved.

It was felt unlikely that the proposal would make much of an impact on the group of mentally ill people for whom it was intended; that is, those who cause most concern to the public, who refuse to accept they are ill and who refuse to take medication.

The Committee recommended 'incremental adjustment' to the statutory powers of guardianship once it had been established why guardianship was not used more often. It also recommended better training for clinicians and social workers to improve their understanding of existing powers.

Discussion

The issues raised by the Royal College of Psychiatrists and the Health Committee inspired an internal review by the Department of Health (1993) and the Secretary of State for

Health's 'ten point plan'. Implementation of the plan included supervision registers and the 1995 Act introducing supervised discharge orders; that is, the medicalisation of guardianship with the Health Committee's proposed 'incremental adjustments'. Additional incentive to introduce supervised discharge orders was given by the publication of the Clunis inquiry report in 1994, with its recommendation for special supervision groups to care for the most disturbed and difficult patients who fulfilled certain criteria in terms of their previous history and refusal of treatment. There is so far, however, no evidence to suggest that these or any of the other measures introduced have had any significant impact on the patients, like Clunis, for whom they are intended.

Setting the debate in context, with the number of homicides, suicides and untoward incidents which have taken place in the five years since 1993, the Health Committee's optimism that a little extra training and a few 'incremental adjustments' to existing powers would tackle the problem seems little short of naive, if not reckless. The Secretary of State's view, following the incident of Ben Silcock in the lions' den in December 1992, and the killing of Jonathan Zito two weeks before, that the pendulum had swung too far in favour of civil liberties, was given expression in her 'ten point plan', and in the subsequent encroachment upon the civil liberties of patients with the introduction of supervision registers and supervised discharge orders, yet without any demonstrable improvements in the provision of community care where it is most fallible.

Now the opportunity has arisen, once again, for a reconsideration of this highly contentious issue. It seems unlikely that the courts will sanction anything other than new statutory powers, clearly and unambiguously expressed, where a patient is being forced to receive treatment in the absence of consent. It is also clear that the passing of such unambiguous statutory powers will be challenged under European law. Creative mechanisms for subverting current legislation in the interests of patients, such as extended leave of absence, have been outlawed.

The most effective method of ensuring that patients continue to take their medication in the community is by providing more *Gemeinschaft* and less *Gesellschaft* (see Introduction, p iv), that is, a full and integrated spectrum of care involving the whole of the community and a full range of facilities, run by people who are able to offer regular and meaningful face-to-face contact, with back-up crisis care available 24 hours a day. In addition, there needs to be a clear and unambiguous recognition that some patients are currently too ill and too dangerous to be living in the community. These patients need to be in hospital until they are ready to be discharged into the care of people living and working in the community, supported by proper facilities and professional supervision and training. Establishing this kind of culture is not simply a matter of one or two adjustments and a bit of additional funding. The entire policy of community care needs to be overhauled with significant new funding and a radical programme of expansion, recruitment and training to meet the needs of difficult and challenging patients. If these patients - patients like Clunis - get proper care and treatment in the community, and are made to feel safe, contained and worthwhile in the community, then the rest will follow, it is suggested, if there is sufficient capacity, funding and determination to make it happen. The need is to transform a system that is currently dysfunctional and dangerous, to one that is effective and safe for patients, carers and the public. Can it be done? Or is belief in such possibilities naive on a spectacular scale?

Flavour of the month to achieve the breakthrough is 'assertive outreach', which has been piloted in some parts of the UK, following studies of it in other parts of the world. Simply put, it involves specialist multidisciplinary teams keeping track of small numbers (10-15) of mentally ill people in the community, monitoring their progress (and whereabouts), and keeping them out of hospital. Reduced admission rates release resources which are then used to fund the assertive outreach schemes.

This is the approach favoured by the Sainsbury Centre for Mental Health in its report, *Keys to Engagement*, reported in the *Guardian* (1998) and the *Health Service Journal* (1998). The report recommends that every health authority in England should pilot assertive outreach, at a total cost of £50m. In the long-term the cost of caring for the 15,000 'socially excluded' severely mentally ill is estimated at £300m. One of the UK areas cited as having implemented assertive outreach successfully is north Birmingham which has five 24 hour crisis home treatment teams, employing more than 70 staff. Another example given is Haringey in north London. Neither area, however, has a particularly clean slate in terms of preventing community care-related homicides, suicides or violent attacks, but perhaps it is too early to judge.

The assertive outreach programmes in England are based on examples studied in Madison, Wisconsin; Keene in New Hampshire; Trieste in Italy; Lower North Shore, Sydney, and in Montreal and Chicago (Mahoney, 1998). One of the central lessons learned in other jurisdictions is the level of commitment and vigour needed to make these schemes work. In Trieste, for example, the programme was fundamentally aided by substantial housing stocks; attempts to translate the approach elsewhere in Italy have not been successful (Jones and Poletti, 1986). It is also essential that inpatient care is integrated as a critical component of the assertive outreach approach, and is not simply substituted by it (Burns and Kent, 1994).

Modern approaches to care in the community are, to some extent, dependent on the new pharmacological developments in the treatment of schizophrenia, with their better side-effect profile than conventional compounds. Currently, however, these treatments are only available in tablet form and cannot be administered by depot injection. There is, therefore, increased pressure and responsibility on the part of patients; the opportunities for misleading carers about medication in tablet form will be increased and will need effective monitoring and supervision by the assertive outreach teams if the patients are to remain compliant in the community.

Conclusion

It is just possible that the necessary improvements to community care delivery can be made using existing legislative powers in conjunction with a much more assertive approach to patient care. The requirements are clear: increased use of guardianship, repeal of the Mental Health (Patients in the Community) Act 1995, a comprehensive, multidisciplinary programme of training in the effective use of the Mental Health Act 1983 and additional funding of some £500m as a basic minimum to resource new 24 hour nursed beds and multidisciplinary teams working pro-actively with small groups of patients. These measures may not be enough. Anything less will be wholly inadequate.

The scale of the problem to be tackled is real, as a call from the organisation Shelter reveals just as this chapter was nearing completion. A man who is now homeless has come to the attention of Shelter. He has been admitted to hospital 26 times in his 'career' so far and is considered to be dangerous. The health authority concerned say they can do nothing for him and refuse to admit him again. Social services have informed Shelter this man is not their responsibility and, even if he was, they have no accommodation for him.

References

Blom-Cooper, L., Hally, H. and Murphy, E. (1995) *One Patient's Mental Health Care 1978-1993*. London: Duckworth.

Burns, T. and Kent, A. (1994) Integrated care is part of the integrated approach (letter). *British Medical Journal* 308: 1235-6.

Department of Health (1993) *Legal Powers on the Care of Mentally Ill People in the Community: Report of the Internal Review*. London: Department of Health.

Dyer, T. (1998) 'Treatment in the community in the absence of consent'. *Psychiatric Bulletin* 22: 73-6.

Exworthy, T. (1995) 'Compulsory care in the community: a review of the proposals for compulsory supervision and treatment of the mentally ill in the community'. *Criminal Behaviour and Mental Health*, 5: 218-41.

Fennell, P. (1996) *Treatment Without Consent; Law, Psychiatry and the Treatment of Mentally Disordered People since 1845*. London: Routledge.

Health Committee of the House of Commons (1993) *Community Supervision Orders*, Vol.1: *Fifth Report*. London: HMSO.

Health Service Journal (1998) Assertive outreach could help mentally ill. 12 March.

Mahoney, J. (1998) Community care is not the work of a single leader (letter). *Health Service Journal* 12 March.

Royal College of Psychiatrists (1987) *Community Treatment Orders - A Discussion Document*. London: Royal College of Psychiatrists.

Royal College of Psychiatrists (1993) *Community Supervision Orders*. Council Report CR 18. London: Royal College of Psychiatrists.

The Guardian (1998) 'Assertive outreach' hope over care in the community. 9 March.

Legal Cases

R v *Hallstrom, ex parte W*; *R* v *Gardner, ex parte L* (No 2) [1986] Q.B 1090. [1986] 2 W.L.R. 883.

CHAPTER THREE

NON-COMPLIANCE

Introduction

This chapter discusses the concept of compliance - initially from a general medical perspective, followed by a more specialised discussion of compliance and mental illness. Chapter four then looks in detail at the homicides committed by community care patients who have been in contact with mental health services where non-compliance was a significant factor. Chapter five discusses a number of key areas in non-compliance which are highlighted in the reports. The range of inquiries under scrutiny takes, as a starting point *The Report of the Inquiry into the Care and Treatment of Christopher Clunis* (Chair: Jean Ritchie QC) in February 1994, and ends with the most recent at the time of publication, *'Sharing The Burden': An independent inquiry into the care and treatment of Desmond Ledgester* (Chair : Mrs V. J. Double) which was published in January 1998. There is, therefore, information contained in inquiry reports over a four-year period, a period which has seen a continued acceleration in psychiatric bed closures and a continuing emphasis placed on providing care and treatment for the severely mentally ill in the community.

The majority, but not all, of the inquiries studied were established in accordance with guidance issued by the Department of Health in 1994 (HSG(94)27), following the Clunis report, guidance which was reaffirmed by the NHS Executive in October 1995 in Chapter 5 of *Building Bridges.*

The present analysis begins with the question, 'what is non-compliance?' and discusses this issue in the overall context of patients, medication and the health service. Discussion proceeds to non-compliance and mental illness.

What is non-compliance?

The issue of non-compliance with treatment, and with medication in particular, is complex and the following brief commentary cannot do more in the context of this report than summarise some recent thinking. Initial observations are, in the main, indebted to a joint report published in 1995 by the Royal Pharmaceutical Society (RPS) and Merck Sharp and Dohme: *From Compliance to Concordance; Achieving Shared Goals In Medicine Taking.*

Research has suggested that as many as 50% of patients do not fully comply with the terms of their prescription (Sackett, 1979), despite medication being the major form of treatment for their illness.

This has dramatic consequences for both the patient and the NHS, resulting in reduced efficacy of drug treatment and the substantial extra financial cost to the health service in terms of having to treat subsequent, avoidable and frequently exacerbated health problems.

The working party established by the RPS reviewed thirty years of literature on patient compliance and published their analysis in 1995. Several recommendations were made for the future training of health care professionals, and it was proposed that a three year programme be initiated, with the general aim of gaining further insight into this problematic area.

A central issue in the joint report is preference for use of the term concordance in place of compliance (or adherence). Although compliance is the term most typically used, it implies that doctors merely give orders which must be followed regarding treatment, and that patients lack the ability to make informed decisions for themselves about their medication. The RPS felt that concordance is a more appropriate word which expresses the equality inherently needed in the patient-prescriber relationship. Only an equal relationship of this sort fosters the development of a 'therapeutic alliance', from which greater concordance can be achieved.

However, as the vast majority of research in the field favours the term *compliance* as the norm, the RPS report continued to use it, and defined *non-compliance* as any 'departure from the intended regimen, likely to reduce the medicine's effectiveness.'

Non-compliance does not, however, usually involve total abstinence from medication. Rather, the patient tends to omit or forget certain doses, or he/she takes a 'drug holiday' before resuming the normal pattern. Drug holidays are a particular cause for concern, as they can lead to severe physiological (or in psychiatry, severe psychological) damage to the patient. It is important to point out, however, by way of qualification, that not all drugs rely on compliance to the same extent in producing effective responses.

A multitude of factors were identified being instrumental in a patient's decision not to comply with medication. These factors were most often dependent upon either individual, familial, cultural or social experiences (past and present) or, as in many cases, a combination of all of these.

Individual factors which have been positively correlated with non-compliance include physical or social vulnerability. This is certainly apparent in the care and treatment of the mentally ill with anti-psychotic drugs. Old age is also a discrete factor, compounded when elderly patients are required, as they often are, to take a variety of drugs, thereby increasing the incidence or prevalence of non-compliance.

It has been noted that as the frequency of medication dosage increases, non-compliance increases accordingly. This can be attributed to the fact that having to adhere to any drug regime is disruptive and can provoke considerable anxiety, with increased dosages leading to further unwanted preoccupation with the disease state.

A standard division was made in the RPS review between motivational causes of non-compliance (based on beliefs and experiences of the patient) and non-compliance which is caused by inadequate recognition by health professionals of the importance of such motivational beliefs.

Additionally, two categories of non-compliance were highlighted: primary, whereby individuals fail even to collect their prescription from the pharmacist (this happens in up to one in five cases); and secondary, whereby the medicine is not taken as intended or as set out on the prescription. Departure from the instructions set out by the doctor or pharmacist can be either intentional, as in the patient disagreeing with the diagnosis and/or treatment course, or unintentional, due to forgetfulness or stress.

Sociological research offers a number of explanations as to what might inform or condition the beliefs patients may have concerning medication. A few examples are:

- Medication is unnatural. It is common for patients to worry about the negative effects of a synthesised, chemical substance on their bodies.
- Worry over physical addiction
- Worry about the danger of acquiring decreased natural immunity over time as the body increases its natural resistance to the medication
- Strong attitudes against drugs
- Scepticism about the actual benefits of the medication prescribed by patients who hold differing views over just how efficient a drug is, and what it can do for them.

These instances are among those highlighted in the RPS report to illustrate why an individual may choose not to comply with treatment, and to emphasise the importance of doctors taking such beliefs seriously and considering them pro-actively and sensitively in consultation with their patients.

Intervention programmes aimed at improving patient compliance are either educational, involving giving information to the patient (for example, the patient information leaflets which are often enclosed with prescribed drugs); or behavioural, concentrating on the patient's lifestyle and how best to gear prescribing practices to it and to the patient. Other techniques include providing the patient with a variety of prompts, such as reminders from friends or relatives to take the medication; or the use of calendar packs or specialised multi-compartment containers. Of course these are only effective interventionist methodologies in cases of unintentional non-compliance and do not really strike at the core, problematic cases. Generally, no long term changes in patient compliance have been reported without the particular intervention being regularly repeated, and overall there has been a widespread failure to reduce significantly the levels of non-compliance in the United Kingdom.

The RPS review of the literature revealed a lack of consensus among researchers over the relationship between compliance and particular diseases and symptoms. There is a paucity of information which might predict the kinds of patient who might be compliant and, conversely, those who are more likely to be non-compliant, and on the particular roles of doctors, nurses and pharmacists in achieving compliance.

Recommendations of note from the RPS review fell into two categories, and included:

1. Research and Development

- New models of patient concordance to be developed and evaluated for use in the NHS.
- New behaviour intervention programmes to be developed.
- Actual medication changes to be brought about, such as combining different medicines to reduce the number of different drugs to be taken; higher doses of drugs (rather than increasing dosage over time) to enable shorter courses of medication; improved tolerability.
- The role of pharmacists to be strengthened, enabling them to make prescribing decisions and to inform patients about pharmaceutical alternatives.
- Consider giving patients more power by allowing them to hold their own records in some form, thereby giving them some ownership and power thus improving their ability to reach their own decisions about treatment with which they feel they could comply.

2. Professional Education and Training

Training is needed on a wider and more detailed scale than at present, ranging from undergraduate to postgraduate level, and covering a variety of health care professionals. The RPS is currently one of the only bodies to have a comprehensive training programme addressing the compliance issue.

In order for these recommendations to be implemented, a research and development strategy using a multidisciplinary approach would need to be adopted, to be included in the NHS's existing research and development programme. The education and training programme would require support from the university and training colleges, as well as the royal colleges and professional societies.

Traditional models of patient non-compliance have focused, simplistically, on the discrepancy between treatment programmes offered by doctors and patients' rejection of them, and have suggested that the problem can be overcome by bringing the patient into line with the scientific, medical way of thinking.

In conclusion, the RPS suggests that concordance should be a goal of medical treatment, which in itself should take into full consideration the beliefs and anxieties of the patient. This means forging an alliance between doctor and patient that would allow for greater harmony and equality between the two, which would result in better compliance because the patient is at the heart of the prescribing process, playing a meaningful part in treatment decisions, rather than being on the receiving end of them.

Non-compliance and psychiatry

This section on non-compliance and psychiatry summarises a paper on improving treatment adherence published recently by Sair et al. (1998). The paper presents the literature on compliance as ideology, before examining strategies to improve patient outcomes if non-compliance is identified as undermining the current regimen.

Unlike the RPS report, which prefers the term 'concordance' to compliance, Sair et al. draw attention to the use of the concept 'adherence', emphasising the need identified by the RPS of the place of the clinician in forming a treatment alliance with the patient.

It is likely that non-compliance in psychiatric patients is more common than in other patients because of the effects of the illnesses or conditions on insight and judgement. Non-compliance is well recognised as a major risk indicator of violence to self or others.

Non-compliance increases inpatient hospital admissions, thereby adding to the financial and personal burden. The number of patients who are reported to be non-compliant ranges between 11-80%, with 48% non-compliant in the first year and 74% within two years. The paper points out that non-compliance is not simply a 'community care' problem, as up to 19% of inpatients do not take their drugs regularly. A survey by Clary et al. (1992) of 253 psychiatric inpatients on the day of discharge reported that not more than half knew the name and dose of the medication, nor why they were taking it, even though they had received group and individual instruction during their stay in hospital.

The reasons for non-compliance in mental illness can be categorised as follows:

- insight into the illness and the effects of medication
- communication between patients and clinicians
- cognitive impairment and comorbidity
- instructions on labels
- dual diagnosis
- adverse effects
- culture, self-determination and stigma

Strategies for improving compliance/adherence are mostly psychoeducational interventions, ranging from giving information, teaching participants about symptoms, increasing patients' and families' awareness of the signs of relapse, to encouraging simple daily rituals, shortening the waiting time before appointments, and involving patients in the decision-making process.

The authors conclude that training is essential yet point to the fact there is no identified funding to deliver this. Neither are there any clinical guidelines specifically aimed at treatment adherence.

References

Clary, C., Dever, A. and Schweizer, E. (1992) 'Psychiatric inpatients' knowledge of medication at hospital discharge'. *Hospital and Community Psychiatry*, 43: 140-4.

Sackett, D.L. and Snow, J.C. (1979) 'The magnitude of compliance and non-compliance'. In Haynes, R.B., Taylor, W.D. and Sackett, D.L. (eds) *Compliance in Health Care*. Baltimore: Johns Hopkins University Press.

Sair, A., Kamaldeep, B., Haq, S. and Strathdee, G. (1998) 'Improving treatment adherence among patients with chronic psychoses'. *Psychiatric Bulletin*, 22: 77-81

CHAPTER FOUR

NON-COMPLIANCE AND THE INDEPENDENT INQUIRIES

Introduction

Of the 35 independent inquiry reports studied since (and including) the Clunis report was published in February 1994, non-compliance with medication was found to be a significant contributory factor in 20 of them (57%). The 20 cases are:

1. Christopher Clunis
2. Michael Buchanan
3. Andrew Robinson (*The Falling Shadow*)
4. John Rous (Newby report)
5. Philip McFadden
6. Stephen Laudat (*The Woodley Team Report*)
7. Kenneth Grey
8. Jason Mitchell
9. Nilesh Gadher
10. Francis Hampshire
11. Richard Burton
12. Anthony Smith
13. Martin Mursell
14. Susan Joughin
15. Paul Smith
16. Doris Walsh
17. Sarah Beynon
18. Damian Witts
19. Norman Dunn
20. Desmond Ledgester

Below are listed those patients in inquiry reports in which non-compliance was not found to be a factor, or in which non-compliance was not examined:

1. Alan Boland
2. Brian Doherty
3. Robert Viner (*The Viner Report*)
4. Shaun Armstrong
5. Raymond Sinclair
6. Kumbi Mabota
7. Keith Taylor (*Caring For The Carer*)
8. Richard Stoker
9. Evan Barry
9. Evan Barry
10. Darren Carr
11. Peter Winship
12. Gilbert Kopernik-Steckel
13. Michael Horner
14. William Scott
15. James Stemp

The following inquiry reports were either published in part only, and do not contain any information which would have been helpful to this study, or were not published at all, in which case information is not available. These cases are not included in our figures.

1. John Renouf (1996, not published)
2. Geoffrey Weaver (1997, not published)
3. Susan Newson (1997, not published)
4. Paul Medley (1997, recommendations only published)

Summary details of the 20 inquiry reports in which non-compliance was a major contributory factor in the events leading to the homicide:

1 CHRISTOPHER CLUNIS

Report of the Inquiry into the Care and Treatment of Christopher Clunis
Jean Ritchie QC, Dr Donald Dick and Richard Lingham
Published 24 February 1994 by North East Thames and South East Thames Health Authorities (HMSO).

Summary

Christopher Clunis (CC) was born in 1963. Both his parents came from Jamaica. He began to show odd behaviour in 1968 and went to stay with his father in Jamaica. CC was subsequently admitted to Bellevue Hospital, Kingston, Jamaica where he was diagnosed as suffering from paranoid schizophrenia. He returned to London the following year and was admitted to various psychiatric hospitals on a number of occasions in the following years. On 20 August 1992, CC was detained under s.3 Mental Health Act 1983 (MHA) and transferred the following day from Kneesworth House to Guys Hospital. He was discharged on 24 December 1992 to accommodation in Haringey. On 17 December 1992, CC stabbed Jonathan Zito, a complete stranger, to death in an unprovoked attack at Finsbury Park tube station. On the day of the homicide an approved social worker visited CC's address unaccompanied, leaving a note asking him to call and see her. He was by then in custody. CC pleaded guilty to manslaughter at the Old Bailey on 28 June 1993 and sent to Rampton Hospital under ss.37/41 MHA 1983.

Medication

CC was known to respond well to medication but there was wide variation in the level and frequency of the doses prescribed. He was sometimes compliant but he almost invariably failed to turn up to outpatient appointments. On the rare occasions when follow-ups in the community were on offer CC often refused to accept them. Successful follow-ups were possible, indeed it was probably only the attendance of the cpn at the Rosemead Hostel to give CC depot injections that kept him on any medication at all. Once in the community he deteriorated. The only highlighted episode of non-compliance was due to CC's disagreement with high doses and refusal to accept depot injections until his medication was reviewed, but court reports prepared in August 1992 point to a history of non-compliance with treatment in the community, relapse and violence.

Chronology

11 August 1988
Discharged from his ninth hospital stay (at Dulwich North Hospital) CC is given an outpatient appointment to attend a depot clinic for injections, but there is no evidence as to whether he attends.

9 June-6 July 1989
At St. Charles' Hospital CC is prescribed a depot injection of clopixol. A doctor notes that he is responding well to treatment, but is aware that he had relapsed after six weeks in the community after his last discharge. CC is admitted under s.3 MHA 1983 to allow for more prolonged treatment.

6-27 July 1989
At Horton Hospital in Surrey his condition improves on medication although it is noted he is likely to become violent under pressure.

27 July-14 November 1989
At St. Charles' Hospital medication is gradually reduced at the suggestion of the Senior Registrar, probably because of staff reports that CC spends most of the day in bed and is very drowsy. From **10 August** a deterioration in his mental state is evident but by the end of **September** the SR describes him as well, feeling that the prescribed medication suits him. On discharge CC is given an outpatient appointment which he does not keep. The inquiry found that no proper arrangements had been put in place for him to receive depot injections (which were to be administered every three weeks).

November 1989-October 1990
CC is resident at the Rosemead Hostel. The failure to arrange depot injections means the prescription for the injection due on **5 December** has to be sent by fax to the cpn. During his stay at Rosemead Hostel, it is recorded that CC accepted his depot injections. It is unclear from records who is prescribing depot injections and this was considered as indicative of poor follow-up procedures. The cpn administered the depot injections and was supposed to evaluate effects and ensure that CC was seen regularly by a doctor to review medication. The cpn was unsuccessful in ensuring that medication was regularly reviewed and this may have contributed to CC's subsequent non-compliance with medication. In addition, he did not see the consultant psychiatrist for months. By **July 1990** the report for CC's emergency case conference refers to the fact that *CC was no longer taking oral medication at a time when his care was breaking down (he had already lost his job and was about to lose his home*). The abuse of staff and residents by CC, and poor personal hygiene, was thought to be related to his deteriorating mental state. A new cpn took over in **September** without a proper handover of the case and he decided that CC should be able to attend a depot clinic, apparently unaware that CC was to leave Rosemead at the request of staff. The inquiry report comments that at this time CC required more supervision, not less. Staff at the Rosemead Hotel failed to ensure that CC kept his outpatient appointments.

9 November 1990
The cpn gives CC his depot injection and notes he is asymptomatic. CC agrees to attend the next clinic on **29 November**. However, CC fails to attend the clinic and also misses the subsequent appointment on **20 December**. On both occasions the cpn visits him and administers the depot injections. CC tells the cpn he does not like the side-effects and wants to see the consultant psychiatrist to arrange a change in medication, but no appointment is made.

4 February 1991
CC again says he wants his medication changed because of the side-effects. The cpn makes an appointment at St. Thomas' Hospital, which CC fails to attend on **22 February**. This means it is now 13 months since he has seen the consultant psychiatrist.

26 February 1991
CC refuses his depot injection unless an outpatient appointment is arranged in order to review his medication. The cpn makes an appointment for six weeks time (at South Western Hospital) and visits CC to give the injection. CC is angry at the delay and again refuses his medication. An appointment is made at a different hospital (St Thomas') for **14 March** and the cpn asks staff at the Jeffrey's Road Hostel to inform CC who, in the meantime, is without medication. Another cpn, concerned at the situation, tries to persuade CC to accept the depot injection. CC still refuses and says he will attend the new appointment and then accept the injection. However, he does not attend as he has been arrested by police on **12 March** after chasing residents round the Jeffrey's road

hostel with a carving knife. No charges are brought by the police. CC is subsequently placed in B&B accommodation. Lambeth Social Services then lose all contact with him for four months, during which time he receives no care and relapses in **July**.

23 July-17 August 1991
CC is on Lloyd Still Ward at St Thomas' Hospital, Lambeth. With no bed available on the locked ward he is contained on an open ward with very high doses of medication, up to 900mgs chlorpromazine four times daily. At this time CC is both psychotic and violent. The cpn doubts the therapeutic value of such high doses and believes it to be for the sole purposes of containment. The rmo disagrees, believing that CC is never unwilling to take his medication while on the ward. However, this belief was based on a further belief that CC never showed signs of wanting to leave the ward. CC goes absent without leave on **17 August**.

17-27 August 1991
CC is now living at Spur House Resettlement Unit. On **27 August** he attacks another resident. At the time of the attack he is not receiving any medication. A doctor, who saw Clunis on **28 August**, comments that the reason for the incident was that CC had not been receiving medication.

4 May 1992
CC is seen by the welfare officer, at Lancelot Andrews House Resettlement Unit. CC tells him he cannot not sleep because he has not had any medication. The welfare officer is concerned but does nothing except arrange for an appointment the next morning. During the night CC attacks another resident with a knife, who has to be taken to hospital.

14 August 1992
CC goes to Kneesworth House Hospital where a doctor writes, 'although his psychosis is coming under control with medication, he shows little insight into the need for continuing treatment. He would not cooperate with treatment outside the hospital and would be likely to relapse. He could again act in a dangerous way if he becomes floridly psychotic.' This observation will be repeated in CC's court report following the homicide.

25 August 1992
As an inpatient at Guy's Hospital CC threatens a doctor when the need for an injection is discussed. The next day CC says he is well and is willing to take his medication. On this basis, and following his good behaviour, he is discharged. CC indicates he does not want any after-care or social services involvement. Social Services accept this as he appears to be taking his medication and indicates he will seek help if feels he needs any.

17 December 1992
Christopher Clunis kills Jonathan Zito at Finsbury Park underground station.

2 MICHAEL BUCHANAN

Report of the Independent Panel of Inquiry Examining the Case of Michael Buchanan
Christopher Heginbotham, Jacqueline Carr, Dr Robert Hale, Thomas Walsh and Linda Warren
Published 4 November 1994 by North West London Mental Health NHS Trust, IKEA Tower, 225 North Circular Road, Brent Park, London NW10 0JQ (0181 830 0033)

Summary

Michael Buchanan was born on 31 July 1964. He was first admitted to a psychiatric hospital in 1983 and was subsequently admitted on a further 12 occasions. He was last admitted on 31 July 1992 to Shenley Hospital under s.37, Mental Health Act 1983. Following a s.117 aftercare meeting on 18 August 1992 he was discharged on 21 August 1992 after 22 days on the ward to a Church Army Hostel. On 10 September 1992, Michael Buchanan entered an underground car park on the Stonebridge Park Estate, Harlesden in north London. In the car park Frederick Graver, a 54 year old former policeman, had just parked his car. Michael Buchanan picked up a piece of wood and attacked him, knocking him to the ground. He hit Frederick Graver about the head with the wood and stamped on his face with great force causing 13 severe multiple fractures to his facial bones. Frederick Graver died in hospital two days later.

Medication

Staff at Shenley Hospital emphasised Michael Buchanan's rapid response to medication. Following discharge, however, MB was known to refuse anti-psychotic medication and other follow-up care, and this had been the case in the days leading up to fatal attack on Frederick Graver. The report criticises the cpn's decision to discharge MB from his caseload shortly before the attack.

Chronology

22 May 1986
MB admitted to Shenley Hospital from Pound Lodge Hostel following aggressive and disturbed behaviour, and refusal to take his medication.

18 October 1986
MB discharges himself against medical advice back to Pound Lodge. An outpatient appointment is made but he absconds without taking any medication.

24 June 1988
Twelve months' probation for burglary with condition that he receives psychiatric treatment.

25 July 1988
Sentenced to six months' probation for deception and theft. Sentenced to three months' imprisonment for theft.

11 November 1988
Probation officer writes to the mental health unit expressing his concern that MB has not yet seen a psychiatrist despite court instructions of 24 June 1988. It is believed that MB is more likely to remain well on release if he receives medication in prison and that if he is released on 23 December without medical treatment he must be considered as a risk.

21 December 1988
MB admitted to Shenley Hospital on s.47 Mental Health Act 1983.

13 March 1989
Discharged to bed and breakfast accommodation. No discharge arrangements from Shenley could be found in the medical records. No cpn or outpatient notes available. Depot medication not administered as cpn is unaware of MB's whereabouts.

25 May 1989
Admitted to Pond Ward CMH (self-referral on advice of probation officer) MB had defaulted on his medication prior to admission. Uncooperative and placed on a s 2 order.

17 August 1989
New admission to Pond Ward, having 'allegedly taken' overdose of the medication he had been discharged with on 15 August 1989.

2 October 1989
MB visited by cpn following discharge from Pond Ward on 23 August, after absconding. Given depot injection.

23 October 1989
MB visited by cpn, who thought he was avoiding depot injection.

4 November 1989-13 February 1990
The cpn had difficulty locating MB and then persuading him to accept depot medication.

27 April 1990
MB discharged from Shenley Hospital. The cpn visits MB who refuses medication.

26 June 1990
The cpn visits MB, who refuses depot injection and refuses to continue treatment. MB asks the cpn not to visit again and is discharged from the cpn's caseload, apparently with the approval of the consultant psychiatrist responsible for MB.

September 1990-June 1991
MB on several charges of actual bodily harm, assessed in Brixton prison, subject to a hospital order under s 37 MHA, admitted to Villa 4, Shenley Hospital, transferred to Pond Ward, absconds, arrested, re-admitted to Pond Ward, assaults staff, sexually disinhibited, abusive, threatening, volatile; vicious attack on a female nurse, absconds again.

14 August 1991
MB is discharged to his flat on the Stonebridge Park Estate.

27 August 1991
Accepts depot medication from his new cpn.

9 December 1991
MB does not keep outpatient appointment for depot medication. The cpn discharges MB from his caseload that day.

14 February 1992
MB sentenced to nine months' imprisonment for burglary.

31 July 1992
MB admitted to Shenley under s 37 MHA. Responds well to medication. His care is discussed on **11 August** on the ward round. He is assessed as not psychotic and complying with treatment, including medication. On **19 August**, further discussion takes place concerning MB's discharge under s 117 MHA. The importance of compliance with medication on discharge is noted.

21 August 1992
MB given depot injection and discharged. Depot injection to be repeated fortnightly.

7 September 1992
The cpn writes to the rmo to say that MB has not kept his appointment to continue treatment following discharge. The cpn discharges MB from his caseload. The next depot injection is due on 14 September.

10 September 1992
Michael Buchanan attacks and kills Frederick Graver

Note

Michael Buchanan was subsequently examined by his rmo at Wormwood Scrubs Prison in November 1992, some two months after the homicide. His conclusion was that MB suffered from schizophrenia, which responded well to antipsychotic drugs. He stated that attempts in the past to continue treatment following discharge from hospital were met with refusal by MB. The inquiry report highlights the fact that staff were well aware of this but the combination of MB's challenging and aggressive behaviour on the wards, and his rapid improvement once on medication, meant that staff were keen to discharge him. He was admitted to hospital 13 times between 1983-1993. The last admission was to a locked ward at Shenley Hospital in July 1992, following transfer from Brixton Prison under s 37 of the Mental Health Act 1983. Despite the potential to treat him for six months, he was discharged after three weeks. Staff felt unable to treat anything other than the symptoms that emerged periodically and emphasised his rapid improvement on medication. MB was viewed as a very difficult patient who manipulated and assaulted others on the ward. After his discharge, he was placed in a hostel which was not geared to coping with his behavioural problems. He was, unsurprisingly, discharged from the hostel within three weeks, because did not comply with the rules. On the following day his cpn could not find him, so he discharged him from his caseload. MB slept rough, stopped taking his medication, and committed several serious and violent crimes to obtain money for drugs, culminating in the fatal attack on Frederick Graver on 10 September 1992.

3 ANDREW ROBINSON

The Falling Shadow: One Patient's Mental Health Care 1978-1993
Sir Louis Blom-Cooper QC, Helen Hally and Professor Elaine Murphy
Published 16 January 1995 by Gerald Duckworth & Co Ltd, The Old Piano Factory, 48 Hoxton Square, London N1 6PB (0171 729 5986)

Summary

Andrew Robinson was born in 1957. He was first admitted to a psychiatric unit in 1977. In 1978, following a conviction for carrying a firearm with intent to endanger the life of a female university student, and assault occasioning actual bodily harm, he was made the subject of a hospital order with restrictions and admitted to Broadmoor Hospital. He was transferred to a local hospital in 1981 and conditionally discharged in 1983. Andrew Robinson was admitted on several occasions to the Edith Morgan Centre (EMC) between 1986 and his last admission on the 9 June 1993, when he was initially detained as an emergency under s 4 Mental Health Act 1983 and then the following day reassessed and detained for treatment.

On 1 September 1993, Georgina Robinson, aged 27, an occupational therapist at the Edith Morgan Centre at Torbay District Hospital, was fatally wounded by Andrew Robinson who was still detained under s 3 MHA. Georgina Robinson died on 7 October 1993. Andrew Robinson pleaded guilty to manslaughter on the grounds of diminished responsibility and was detained under a hospital order with restrictions under ss 37/41 MHA and readmitted to Broadmoor Hospital.

Medication

Andrew Robinson (AR) was first admitted to Broadmoor Hospital in 1978 following an attack on his ex-girlfriend with a firearm (index offence). He received two different diagnoses while there: personality disorder and then schizophrenia. After his release he was in and out of hospital. AR had four separate admissions to the Edith Morgan Centre (EMC), each one preceded by a medication-free period. It was known among AR's health care workers that without compulsory powers to treat him, or effective monitoring of his care, he would not comply with treatment, including medication.

Chronology

March 1985
All of AR's medication is stopped. The notes of the responsible doctor contain no explanation for this. However, at the time, the psychiatrist preferred the diagnosis of personality disorder to schizophrenia, which had previously been the diagnosis preferred by those who had assessed him since his first admission to Broadmoor in 1978.

25 April 1986
AR is detained under s 3 MHA at Moorhaven Hospital, following an incident in which he bought a knife and behaved in a disturbed manner in his accommodation. He is placed on stelazine and melleril but by **30 April** doctors stop this medication and no rationale for this is given in the medical notes. AR continues to be off medication for the remainder of his stay at Moorhaven, until **17 September**.

18 November 1986
AR is admitted to Exminster Hospital in Exeter as an informal patient. He has not received medication for 18 months prior to his admission. Staff record him as very aggressive on the ward and he is given chlorpromazine. Eight days later AR discharges himself contrary to medical advice.

29 November 1986
AR is admitted to the EMC under s 4 MHA, later converted to a s 2 admission. He is put on antipsychotic medication but regularly protests and attempts to have the dosage reduced or the prescription altered, in spite of the evidence which suggests that any reductions made lead to a deterioration in his condition.

22 April 1987
AR is considered to have 'settled down', so a community placement order is made to Cypress Rehabilitation Hostel. AR reports his aims are to live independently of any agency connected to mental health and to come off medication, as he believes it controls his thoughts.

22 May 1987
The s 3 MHA order lapses and AR leaves Cypress Hostel. He moves to Exeter. All medication is discontinued.

18 December 1987
AR is readmitted to the EMC under s 2. On **5 January** he is restarted on depot medication after refusing clopixol.

19 January 1988
Staff record difficulties with medication administration and the note made reads, 'accepting medication after some argument'.

9 May 1988
AR is readmitted informally to the EMC after refusing to take his medication. He is formally discharged on **24 June** and receives no further medication.

20 July 1988
The rmo notes that AR has not had any medication since leaving the EMC.

2 August 1988
The cpn assesses AR at a B&B in Paignton. He refuses all medication and does not take any for the next five months.

11 November 1988
AR is admitted under s 2 to the EMC, following non-compliance. On admission, he is hallucinating and is very unwell. AR's father had written to the rmo to inform him of his deterioration.

9 June 1992
The rmo recommends removal of the guardianship order and the halving of medication. By **17 July** the guardianship order has been removed. AR is only reluctantly accepting small doses of medication.

22 September 1992
The rmo agrees to reduce clopixol to three-weekly doses instead of the usual fortnightly after AR complains about the side-effects. It is recognised that monitoring will be needed as the new dose prescribed (actually 150mg every two weeks) is half his normal dose.

22 October 1992
An enrolled mental nurse reports problems in persuading AR to accept the full depot dose (clopixol), and only administers half the required dose.

12 November 1992
Continuing to decrease full dose.

9 December 1992
AR refuses dose of depot injection.

4 January 1993
AR refuses his depot injection. He states that he no longer needs a 'straitjacket'. It is decided that there is no further indication for the medication to be restarted.

25 January 1993
AR has been without medication for six weeks.

1 September 1993
Andrew Robinson kills EMC occupational therapist Georgina Robinson.

Note

The authors of the report believe that every effort should have been made to ensure that medication was taken continuously by Andrew Robinson.

4 JOHN ROUS

Report of the Inquiry into the Circumstances Leading to the Death of Jonathan Newby (A Volunteer Worker)
Nicola Davies QC, Richard Lingham, Clifford Prior and Professor Andrew Sims
Published 26 July 1995 by Oxfordshire Health, Old Road, Headington, Oxford OX3 7LF (01865 741741)

Summary

John Rous was born in 1946. He was first admitted to a psychiatric hospital in 1965 for an amphetamine psychosis, when a diagnosis of personality disorder was made. He had several further admissions under the provisions of the Mental Health Act 1959. He had a street life of some twenty years before he took up residence in Jacqui Porter House, run by the Oxford Cyrenians, in August

1992. Jonathan Newby began working for the Cyrenians as a volunteer in April 1993 and was the only person on duty when he was attacked and stabbed by John Rous in the office of Jacqui Porter House. He was 22 years old when he died. John Rous subsequently admitted manslaughter on the grounds of diminished responsibility and was sent to Broadmoor Hospital under ss 37/41 Mental Health Act 1983.

Medication

If he felt a dose of neuroleptic medication was too high, John Rous (JR) would not comply with treatment. In principle, he received depot medication by injection every two to three weeks from a nurse, but was abusing benzhexol, which was also prescribed. JR's condition was known to deteriorate towards the end of the period between injections. He was due to receive an injection on **5 October 1993**, but this was postponed by the psychiatrist and rescheduled for **11 October**, due to an unexpected professional commitment. JR was known to have been annoyed by this. The homicide took place on **9 October**.

5 PHILIP McFADDEN

Report of the Enquiry into the Care and Treatment of Philip McFadden
Dr James Dyer, Dr Elizabeth McCall-Smith, John Sutherland and Jamie Malcolm
Published 7 August 1995 by the Scottish Office, Department of Health, Room 29D, St Andrew's House, Edinburgh EH1 3DG (0131 556 8400)

Summary

Philip McFadden was born in 1975. He began to show signs of mental illness in 1990 and was, for eight months, a patient in the adolescent unit of Gartnavel Royal Hospital. He continued to have medication and psychiatric contact for the next two years. He was living with his family and his mother contacted the GP practice several times on 17 June 1994, the date of the homicide, concerned about his mental state. The police went to the family home, a visit which resulted in the death of a 28 year old police constable, Lewis Fulton, stabbed by Philip McFadden, and a knife wound to the other policeman involved. Philip McFadden was to have been tried on charges including murder and attempted murder but, at the High Court in Edinburgh in September 1994, was found insane in bar of trial and was sent to the State Hospital at Carstairs under s 174 of the Criminal Procedure (Scotland) Act 1975.

Medication

Philip McFadden (PM) developed schizophrenia at the age of 14 and received treatment as an inpatient from the adolescent psychiatry unit at the Gartnavel Royal Hospital in Glasgow. He also received two years follow-up treatment, and assertive attempts were made to keep him in treatment when he later opted out of it. Two minor episodes of previous violent behaviour were recorded while he was an inpatient at Gartnavel (not specified in the report). He was not considered to be a dangerous patient, and after he stopped taking his medication he was not seen by psychiatric services again until the homicide. Only his family knew that without medication he had become acutely and severely disturbed in both behaviour and thought.

Chronology

2 July 1993
His community psychiatric nurse (cpn) notes that PM has become increasingly reluctant to take his medication (injection of fluphenazine decanoate, 50mgs fortnightly) but accepts an injection on this date.

16 July 1993
The cpn visits PM at home to offer medication which he refuses. PM's non-compliance is reported to his GP.

20 July 1993
The cpn returns to PM's house and medication is again refused. A meeting is subsequently arranged for the cpn, PM, PM's mother and a consultant psychiatrist at the adolescent unit of the Southern General Hospital, Glasgow. Neither PM nor his mother attend. The consultant psychiatrist writes to PM's GP expressing concern over his non-compliance, and informing him that a nurse therapist would take over the cpn's role and try to persuade PM to take medication.

4 August 1993
The therapist writes to PM to inform him of an impending domiciliary visit on the **10 August.** He makes the visit but PM is out. The whole procedure is later repeated. He informs PM by post of the intended visit on **25 August**. He attends but PM is again out. He visits again two days later, but no one is at home. He sends a letter requesting a meeting on the **3 September** but the appointment is not kept. This happens again, with a meeting requested for the **5 November**, but the appointment is not kept.

18 November 1993
PM is discharged from the adolescent psychiatry unit as he has turned 18 and is referred to the general psychiatry unit.

6 December 1993
PM is seen at his GP's surgery by a GP trainee and also seen on **29 March 1994**. On both occasions the nurse practitioner tries to persuade PM to restart his medication. The GP trainee records that, otherwise, there is nothing to be concerned about.

17 June 1994
Philip McFadden kills PC Lewis Fulton.

Note

The inquiry noted that PM was young and had difficulty in accepting his illness. This, therefore, was felt to contribute to his non-compliance. Considerable effort was felt to have been made to keep PM in contact with psychiatric services and restart him on medication.

6 STEPHEN LAUDAT

The Woodley Team Report: Report of the Independent Review Panel to East London and The City Health Authority and Newham Council

Len Woodley QC, Ken Dixon, Vivien Lindow, Dr Oyedeji Oyebode, Tom Sandford and Stephen Simblet

Published 25 September 1995 by East London and The City Health Authority, Tredegar House, 97-99 Bow Road, London E3 2AN (0181 983 2900)

Summary

Stephen Laudat was born in 1968. His mother suffered from mental illness. He was jailed for four years in 1991 for thefts and robberies, one involving a knife. His mental health deteriorated in prison and he was transferred under ss 47/49 Mental Health Act 1983, initially to the Interim Secure Unit at Hackney Hospital and, in June 1992, to Kneesworth House Hospital. He was discharged from Kneesworth House on his earliest release date in December 1993. In July 1994 he stabbed to death Bryan Bennett, aged 56, at a day centre in Newham which both attended. In December 1994, Stephen Laudat was sent to Rampton Hospital under ss 37/41 after he admitted manslaughter on the grounds of diminished responsibility.

Medication

The good quality social care that Stephen Laudat (SL) received was undermined by the poor quality of his health care. The problem presented by SL's non-compliance meant that medication was discontinued on discharge as a pragmatic decision. Staff recognised the likelihood of a relapse in the community without medication but failed to ensure adequate monitoring of his condition which should have been considered an essential component following the decision to discontinue medication. SL's non-compliance was persistent and may have been exacerbated by his dislike of his responsible medical officer.

Chronology

27 February 1991
While serving a prison sentence at HMP Wormwood Scrubs following a number of incidents involving shoplifting, SL punches a prison officer (not the first assault on prison staff by him). Following the assault a diagnosis of schizophreniform psychosis, probably drug-induced, is made and he is found unfit for punishment. He is admitted to the prison health care centre and prescribed oral chlorpromazine. SL refuses this, so the drug is prescribed intra-muscularly. He assaults a medical officer the next day and is again prescribed chlorpromazine intra-muscularly. On the same day (**28 February**) he is transferred to HMP Brixton, where the diagnosis is changed to paranoid psychosis and a prescription of haloperidol by depot is made. There are numerous acts of violence against prison staff during this time.

8 March 1991
SL is found unfit for prison discipline after an attack on prison staff. He is prescribed haloperidol decanoate.

18 March 1991
Some improvement in his condition is reported and he is described as 'improved mentally and accepting haloperidol orally'. SL is diagnosed as suffering from paranoid schizophrenia. When the prison medical officer prepares a court report, he states that SL is symptom free and makes no medical recommendation.

29 July 1991
The dose of oral haloperidol is reduced.

1 August 1991
SL is transferred to HMP Blundeston. His medication is gradually discontinued.

22 January 1992
SL is transferred to HMP Wandsworth because he seems to be relapsing. Due to his mental state he is admitted to the prison health care centre on arrival and treated with chlorpromazine. It is reported that SL is mostly non-compliant. On **5 February** SL is believed to be hallucinating and deluded, but refuses treatment. A few days later he is seen by a consultant psychiatrist at East Ham Memorial Hospital (EHMH), with a view to transfer. The consultant psychiatrist notes that SL shows good response to medication but the psychiatrist does not agree to the transfer to EHMH hospital due to SL's history of violence. SL is then referred to Hackney Hospital. He is seen by a senior registrar in forensic psychiatry who concludes that SL's relapse in prison was due to the cessation of treatment with medication. He advises a transfer to the Hospital under ss 47/49.

23 March 1992
SL is admitted to the Interim Secure Unit at Hackney Hospital. He assaults a patient on the day of admission. A diagnosis of paranoid schizophrenia is made and SL is prescribed neuroleptic medication.

18 June 1992
SL is admitted to Kneesworth House Hospital. Throughout the initial assessment period SL appears pleasant to staff and is compliant with medication. However, SL soon requests to come off medication SL was to tell the inquiry panel that he was concerned at that time about the side-effects of the medication. His medication is changed and he reports that he feels better but still experiencing some side-effects. One of SL's main concerns was that the neuroleptic medication made him impotent. The rmo anticipates from his discussions with SL that he will not continue medication when he leaves hospital, so the plan is to discontinue it so that he can be monitored before discharge.

17 September 1992.
SL's medication is stopped; subsequently no change in his mental state is recorded.

25 November 1993
At the s 117 aftercare planning meeting SL's mental state is reviewed and it is noted that there are insufficient grounds to warrant detention beyond the end of the restriction order which is due to expire on **6 December**. The ward manager expresses his fear of a possible relapse if SL remains without medication and believes he poses a danger to himself and others in such circumstances. The meeting notes that SL's insight into his illness has decreased and there has been a noticeable increase in aggressive attitude. A recommendation to continue the rehabilitation process is made. It is unclear from the meeting whether SL is willing accept social services support. SL had already expressed his clear dislike of the rmo and a reluctance to comply with outpatient appointments.

27 July 1994
Stephen Laudat kills Brian Bennett at the Worland Centre.

Note

The inquiry report criticised the after-care arrangements for Stephen Laudat as deficient. The rmo was over-stretched and SL refused to see her. The decision to discontinue the medication was found to be acceptable only if sufficient monitoring in the community were to replace it. This did not happen.

7 KENNETH GREY

The Grey Report: Report of the Independent Inquiry Team into the Care and Treatment of Kenneth Grey
Jane Mishcon, Dr Donald Dick, Nicholas Welch, Antony Sheehan and Jane Mackay
Published 1 November 1995 by East London and The City Health Authority, Tredegar House, 97-99 Bow Road, London E3 2AN (0181 983 2900)

Summary

Kenneth Grey was born in 1970. From the age of about 13, he started to use cannabis and then began to steal in order to buy drugs. The majority of his convictions were for burglary and theft. He had three convictions for offences involving violence. In June 1994, Kenneth Grey appeared in court charged with shoplifting (while on bail for earlier offences), and one charge of common assault. Prior to sentencing he was the subject of extensive probation assessments which indicated he had a serious drug problem.

While in custody at Pentonville Prison, his behaviour began to cause concern until, in October 1994, he was seen by one of the prison medical officers. By this time he was expressing grandiose and delusional ideas and in mid-October he was seen by a locum consultant psychiatrist from the Intensive Care Unit at Hackney Hospital, who did not consider him as mentally ill at that time. Kenneth Grey had no prior history of mental illness. His health continued to deteriorate and by mid-November he had become threatening towards staff and other prisoners, and was displaying increasingly bizarre and grandiose ideas. He was seen at Pentonville by a forensic psychiatrist who considered him to be floridly mentally ill and he was transferred to Hackney Hospital on 23 November 1994 under s 47 of the Mental Health Act 1983. However, the s 47 order was replaced two days later by a s 2 order, under the mistaken belief that the s 47 expired on Kenneth Grey's earliest date of release with remission (i.e. 25 November 1994).

On the afternoon of 2 December 1994, the s 2 order was discharged almost immediately prior to his transfer from the secure ward to an open ward. Within two hours of arriving on the open ward, he went missing from the Hospital and never returned.

On the evening of the 1 January 1995, Kenneth Grey killed his mother, apparently following an argument with her about religion. He was arrested immediately and it is clear that he was psychotic at the time of the homicide. He was charged with the murder of his mother and on 25 July 1995 he appeared at the Old Bailey where his guilty plea on the grounds of diminished responsibility was accepted. Expert psychiatric evidence was called by both the prosecution and the defence, but the sentencing judge was apparently persuaded by prosecution evidence that Kenneth Grey was suffering from a drug induced psychosis at the time of the murder and that he was no longer showing any signs of mental illness.

Kenneth Grey was sentenced to seven years' imprisonment, but leave was obtained from the Attorney General to refer sentence to the Court of Appeal on the ground that it was unduly lenient.

Medication

Kenneth Grey (KG) had a history of non-compliance. Anti-psychotic drugs worked well in reducing his aggressive behaviour. He also suffered from occasional epileptic fits and was irregular in taking anti-convulsant medication. He also had a history of drug abuse. The trial judge accepted that he committed manslaughter during a drug-induced psychosis.

Chronology

11 November 1994
While in Pentonville Prison KG underwent a number of assessments. He had been seen on **14 October** and assessed as not mentally ill. A second assessment had taken place on **11 October** by the duty doctor, who thought KG 'obviously deluded' and he was admitted to hospital. He initially refused oral medication but by **17 November** he had accepted medication and had calmed down. KG was admitted under s 47 MHA to Hackney Hospital.

22 November 1994
Medical notes record that KG was refusing oral medication and that he 'needs clopixol acuphase 150mg'. He is given a long-lasting sedation-injection for the transfer to Hackney Hospital.

2 December 1994
KG absconds from Hackney Hospital having being simultaneously discharged from a s 2 order and transferred as a voluntary patient to an open-ward. His symptoms had been responding well during his stay at Hackney Hospital, but flared up again after his departure. KG is reported as using illicit drugs during next few weeks.

1 January 1995
Kenneth Grey kills his mother.

8 JASON MITCHELL

The Case of Jason Mitchell: Report of the Independent Panel of Inquiry
Sir Louis Blom-Cooper QC, Dr Adrian Grounds, Pat Guinan, Anne Parker and Michael Taylor
Published 27 March 1996 by Gerald Duckworth & Co Ltd, The Old Piano Factory, 8 Hoxton Square, London N1 6PB (0171 729 5986)

Summary

Jason Mitchell was born in 1970. He was seen by a psychiatrist on a number of occasions while he was serving a period of two years' youth custody for robbery and other offences. In 1990 he attacked a cleaner at St Barnabas Church in Epsom, Surrey and was charged with attempted murder and other offences. He subsequently pleaded guilty at the Central Criminal Court to common assault and possession of offensive weapons (two knives). He was made the subject of a hospital order with restrictions under ss 37/41 of the Mental Health Act 1983. In May 1994 he moved to shared accommodation run by MIND in Felixstowe but, following disruptive behaviour, was readmitted to Eastern House as an informal patient. On 9 December 1994 he left and failed to return. On 20 December 1994 he was arrested following the discovery by police of the bodies of his father, aged 54, and neighbours Arthur and Shirley Wilson, both aged 65. In July 1995 Jason Mitchell was sentenced to three terms of life imprisonment for manslaughter on the grounds of diminished responsibility. On 9 May 1996 he successfully appealed against his sentence and was instead made the subject of a hospital order with restrictions under ss 37/41, Mental Health Act 1983.

Medication

There was some confusion over Jason Mitchell's original diagnosis. Some clinicians diagnosed schizophrenia but others thought he suffered from a drug-induced psychosis. This resulted in confusion about appropriate medication and led to the final decision that antipsychotic medication be discontinued. This had serious consequences. JM was aware that he wasn't well without medication and despite many staff suspecting this to be the case it was decided that medication should not be restarted. JM himself thought that if he had been on medication the homicides would not have been committed.

Chronology

May-June 1990
On Elgar Ward, West Park Hospital, JM is treated with droperidol (oral) and depixol (injection) for six weeks. This leads to an improvement in his positive symptoms but he refuses to take the medication any more. Six weeks after the cessation of treatment, his symptoms return, so the medication is restarted.

June 1991
A reduction in antipsychotic medication is noted as leading to a deterioration in his behaviour.

3 September 1991
A Mental Health Review Tribunal is held and recommends that JM be moved to an open ward and that his medication be reduced and then discontinued as he is not considered to be mentally ill. He

is subsequently moved to an open ward but his behaviour becomes hostile and he reports hallucinations and delusions.

October 1991-February 1992
JM is transferred back to Drummond Ward and medication is reduced in line with the MHRT decision. JM objects to the continuation of medication due to the side-effects and he also feels he does not need it. Medication is therefore stopped. Over the next three months his behaviour deteriorates.

February - March 1992
Depixol is recommended as JM is reporting hallucinations and classical psychotic phenomena. In March 1992 haldol is prescribed and much improvement is reported during the following months.

4 August 1993
In St. Clements Hospital in Ipswich JM is reported as responding well and no behaviour problems are recorded. The dosage of haldol is reduced and then discontinued. JM's mood had stabilised, so the original diagnosis of schizophrenia is questioned, and a possible diagnosis of drug-induced psychosis is considered.

August 1993-December 1994
Medication is never reinstated in spite of JM often reporting hallucinations, delusions, paranoia and presenting with serious behavioural problems following his discharge in **May 1994** to accommodation in Felixstowe and subsequent readmission to Easton House as an informal patient. He repeatedly absconds from the ward.

9 December 1994
JM leaves Easton House and does not return.

12 December 1994
Jason Mitchell kills Arthur and Shirley Wilson.

17/18 December 1994
Jason Mitchell kills his father, Robert Mitchell.

9 NILESH GADHER

Report of the Independent Inquiry Team into the Care and Treatment of Nilesh Gadher
His Honour John Main QC, Dr John Wilkins, David Pope and Steven Manikon
Published 22 April 1996 by Ealing, Hammersmith and Hounslow Health Authority, 1 Armstrong Way, Southall, UB2 4SA (0181 893 0303)

Summary

Nilesh Gadher was born in 1958. He qualified as a pharmacist and worked in this capacity for about five years. He was first referred to a psychiatrist in 1984 when a diagnosis of paranoid schizophrenia was made. In May 1995 he was charged with forging prescriptions and placed on probation. The following year he was struck off the pharmaceutical register. Gadher was admitted to hospital on three occasions under the provisions of the Mental Health Act 1983.

On 6 September 1994 Nilesh Gadher ran over and killed 27 year old Sanita Kaura, a complete stranger. He was found unfit to plead at the Old Bailey on 21 July 1995 and sent to a special hospital.

Medication

Medication was an important part of Nilesh Gadher's treatment but he had a history of non-compliance, particularly with regard to depot injections. His carers therefore relied on oral medication, which made it more difficult for them to monitor except when he was an inpatient or was attending the day hospital, where there could be some supervision. On discharge the arrangement was that he would collect monthly prescriptions from his GP. The subsequent inquiry into the care and treatment of NG made the seemingly obvious recommendation that care programme approach documentation should include information as to the nature of a patient's medication as a matter of course, and that carers should be alerted to signs of relapse. Non-compliance, it says, should be recognised as a significant pointer to relapse.

Chronology

April 1986
NG's first admission to hospital, in Wales, under s 3 MHA. He remains in hospital until **July**, then continues with medication and is seen by his GP and as an outpatient at West Middlesex Hospital in London.

7 February 1987
NG assaults his father. He refuses all medication when seen by his GP and social worker. NG's family forms the view that he is reluctant to accept medication because he dislikes injections. NG indicates a willingness to accept oral medication in hospital as an alternative to compulsory admission, but stops taking his medication as soon as he is discharged.

November-December 1991
Following an assault on a police officer NG is admitted to West Middlesex Hospital under s 3. Charges are later dropped by the police. NG does not settle in hospital and is inclined to appeal against the order for compulsory admission. Towards the end of the section, he stops taking his medication and his condition deteriorates, so a further compulsory admission is considered. He punches a junior doctor who is examining him for this purpose.

1993
NG is considered to be making progress throughout the year and appears to be taking his medication, although his family think he is not taking it. In **October** he is taken off the s.117 register and his social work file is closed.

December 1993
After an overdose of paracetamol NG is admitted to hospital. He tells the doctor who examines him that he had previously been lying to doctors about his compliance and had been non-compliant for 18 months because he felt there was nothing wrong with him and he didn't like the side-effects of the drugs prescribed. While in hospital he occasionally indicates that he will not take his medication once discharged, so depot injections are considered but not given as NG is unwilling to accept them.

NG is told that if does not accept medication he will be sectioned. The rmo feels that as NG is compliant with oral medication he is not sectionable and can be safely discharged to continue treatment at a day hospital. The rmo requests a care programme approach meeting. [The inquiry panel stated the view that NG may well have been sectionable at this time, but a misunderstanding in relation to the MHA 1983 led to the erroneous conclusion that NG did not meet the criteria for compulsory admission].

March 1994
NG is discharged to a day hospital and is discharged from the day hospital on **10 June** and referred to Heston Work Centre. A cpa meeting does not take place until **28 June**. This meeting is described as a 'travesty of a cpa meeting' by the inquiry report. Arrangements for discharge were that NG should obtain his monthly prescriptions from his GP with outpatient reviews. These reviews were subsequently carried out by a senior house officer with limited experience, a situation described by the inquiry report as unsatisfactory, given that supervision under the care programme approach is the responsibilty of the consultant psychiatrist.

August 1994
NG visits his GP and is given a repeat prescription. The GP records in his notes that NG appears to be well. After this consultation there is a marked deterioration in his condition. NG informs the subsequent inquiry panel that he ceased taking his medication in **June** or **July 1994.** The manager of Heston Work Centre reports NG's inappropriate behaviour to the day hospital. The rmo wants NG's social worker to visit, but his social worker is on leave from **6-30 August** and no specific arrangements for holiday cover have been made.

17 August 1994
The community psychiatric nurse sees NG at the Centre after he complains about radio noise. He had previously seen NG on **11 August** and sees no reason to change his view that he is doing well and complying with medication.

6 September 1994
NG kills Sanita Kaura by running her over in a car park.

Note

The inquiry report concludes that the tragedy probably occurred because NG was out of hospital and driving a car when he was not taking his medication. The view was expressed that he might have been compliant with his medication if a failed management plan had not been relied upon, and if a more assertive plan for ensuring compliance (for example, imposing depot injections) had been implemented. It was considered predictable that NG would stop taking oral medication and would become unwell and possibly violent.

10 FRANCIS HAMPSHIRE

The Hampshire Report: Report of the Independent Inquiry Team into the Care and Treatment of Francis Hampshire

Jane Mishcon, Dr Donald Dick, Ian Milne, Paul Beard and Jane Mackay

Published 10 May 1996 by Redbridge and Waltham Forest Health Authority, West Wing, 713 Eastern Avenue, Ilford, Essex IG2 7SJ (0181 518 2299)

Summary

Frank Hampshire was born in 1933 and he married Catherine in 1957. They were both teachers. There was no overtly serious problem with his mental health until about 1983/4. In June 1985 he was referred by his GP to the psychiatric services at Goodmayes Hospital. Over the next nine years he was admitted to hospital on two occasions (once under s 2 of the Mental Health Act 1983). He was also seen as an outpatient and was visited by a community psychiatric nurse.

At about midnight on 31 May 1994, Frank Hampshire killed his wife, aged 62, in a frenzied attack, stabbing her over 300 times in the head and neck.. On the 5 December 1994, at the Central Criminal Court, his plea of guilty to manslaughter on the grounds of diminished responsibility was accepted and he was detained in Rampton Hospital under ss 37/41 Mental Health Act 1983.

Medication

Francis Hampshire's illness was characterised by his persistent minimising of his symptoms, refusing admission to hospital and non-attendance at outpatient appointments when unwell. He often took medication when it was first prescribed and then stopped as soon as he began to feel better. There is strong evidence that FH responded quickly to adequate treatment. The inquiry report placed responsibility for the homicide with FH, but criticised services for not heeding warning signs and, in particular, for allowing FH to dictate the terms of his own treatment.

Chronology

10 January 1986

A domiciliary visit is made to FH and following this visit the doctor who attends writes in a letter to FH's GP that he would benefit from chlorpromazine, but given his history of non-compliance he would probably not take it.

20 April 1993

FH attends an outpatient clinic and a diagnosis of paranoid illness is made. FH refuses to consider medication.

10 May 1993

After another domiciliary visit to FH it is concluded that he would benefit from inpatient care and medication via depot injection, but that he is not sectionable.

17 February 1994

FH is seen as an outpatient. Having already looked up the side-effects of depixol and sulpiride, he is adamant that he will not take them again. He begs the doctor for diazepam.

2 March 1994
It is clear to the rmo that FH is not taking his medication. He refuses lithium and ECT, both recommended by the rmo.

25 May 1994
FH stops taking the anti-depressants prescribed and claims to a disapproving doctor whom Mrs Hampshire has called for advice, that his GP has endorsed this decision. Although sceptical, the doctor does not assess FH in person, nor does she inform other staff or FH's GP about what has happened.

31 May 1994
Francis Hampshire kills Catherine Hampshire.

12 RICHARD JOHN BURTON

Report of the Independent Inquiry into the Treatment and Care of Richard John Burton
Hugh Chapman, Malcolm Ashman, Oluwafemi Oyebode and Brian Rogers
Published 10 October 1996 by Leicestershire Health Authority, Leicestershire Health HQ Building, Gwendolen Road, Leicester, Leicestershire LE5 4QF (0116 273 1173)

Summary

Richard Burton was born on 17 January 1964. He first came into contact with psychiatric services in March 1983, when he was admitted as an informal patient to Scalebor Park Hospital with symptoms of depression, while studying at Leeds University. The psychiatric diagnosis at this time was endogenous depression and it was also concluded that 'he is anxious, schizoid and self critical'. Following his discharge from Scalebor Park Hospital he returned to Leicester and regularly attended the day hospital at Leicester General Hospital until August 1984. In August 1987 he was admitted to Leicester General after taking an overdose, and discharged in September. He then attended the Woodlands Day Hospital between 8 September and 21 September 1987. Following his return from Leeds, Richard Burton worked in a number of clerical or manual jobs and began a relationship with a woman that lasted until in March 1995. In April 1995 he was diagnosed by his GP as suffering from 'clinical depression'. On 5 May, he was treated for an overdose at Leicester Royal Infirmary and an outpatient appointment was made for him for 24 May. Richard Burton killed his landlady on 11 May 1995 and subsequently pleaded guilty at Leicester Crown Court to manslaughter on the grounds of diminished responsibility, and was made the subject of a hospital order with restrictions under ss 37/41 of the Mental Health Act 1983.

Medication

Forensic psychiatric reports presented in court at the trial of Richard Burton (RB) suggested that RB had been engaging in violent fantasies since early adult life and that the violent attack on his landlady had been on his mind for at least three weeks prior to the incident. The subsequent inquiry report noted his history of failure to comply with treatment plans formulated for him. There are, additionally, many instances of self-harm and overdose.

Chronology

4 March 1983
RB is informally admitted to Scalebor Park Hospital. The initial diagnosis records him as 'anxious, schizoid and self-critical'. He is prescribed 125 mgs clomipramine daily and is discharged on **22 April**.

5 May 1983
RB is seen by his GP in Leicester. His medication is reduced to 100mgs clomipramine daily and he is given given 120 capsules.

June 1983 - January 1984
RB sees his GP 13 times. Over this period his medication is gradually reduced until it is eventually discontinued.

April - August 1984
Over this four month period RB regularly attends the day hospital at Leicester General Hospital. In the last month of this contact with mental health services his attendance is poor.

27 August 1987
RB is admitted to Ward 33 of Leicester General Hospital, following an overdose of 80 paracetamol tablets. A diagnosis of depressive personality disorder is made. It is thought that psychotropic medication is not indicated as necessary in this case. A significant portion of the nursing notes were subsequently reported as missing, so it was not possible for the inquiry to assess in detail the nursing care he received during this admission.

25 April 1995
Following the break-up of his long-standing relationship with his girlfriend, RB attends his GP's surgery where he is diagnosed as suffering from clinical depression and is prescribed 20 mg fluoxetine daily and is given 30 tablets. The GP prescribes fluoxetine (prozac) because of its safety in overdose and its good side-effect profile. In evidence to the inquiry, the GP stated that he was aware of reports that fluoxetine might induce violent behaviour.

5 May 1995
RB is seen at Leicester Royal Infirmary after an attempt to overdose on lemsip. He informs a doctor that he had overdosed on 17 fluoxetine tablets the previous day. If true, this meant that RB would not have taken the prescribed dosage of fluoxetine between **5 May** and the date of the homicide (**11 May**).

11 May 1995
Richard Burton kills his landlady, Janice Symons.

11 ANTHONY SMITH

Report of the Inquiry into the Care of Anthony Smith

Professor Sir John Wood, Mr Malcolm Asham, Dr Cyril Davies, Dr Huw Lloyd and Mrs Kate Locket

Published 24 October 1996 by Southern Derbyshire Health Authority, Derwent Court, Stuart Street, Derby, Derbyshire DE1 2FZ (01332 626300)

Summary

Anthony Smith began to show symptoms of mental illness in his early twenties. In June 1995 he was diagnosed as a paranoid schizophrenic and admitted as an inpatient to Derby City General Hospital. This was his first contact with the psychiatric services. On 6 July, following a period of leave, and against the wishes of his father, Anthony Smith was discharged. Back at the family home Anthony failed to take his medication, and five weeks later killed his mother and half-brother in a brutal knife attack. On 6 March 1996, at Nottingham Crown Court, he was ordered to be detained without limit of time in Rampton Hospital after pleading guilty to manslaughter on the grounds of diminished responsibility.

Medication

Anthony Smith improved quickly on medication but was reluctant to take it, particularly once his condition had improved. He described the medication as unpleasant. The inquiry report highlights the difficulties posed by the system for patients who are admitted voluntarily, but who would be sectioned under the Mental Health Act 1983 if they tried to discharge themselves, but who then improve and are not, therefore, considered sectionable. The report suggests that the criteria should be: 'would that patient, if an Order had been in place, have been discharged from it at the current stage of improvement?'

Chronology

15 June 1995

Anthony Smith (AS) is admitted as a voluntary inpatient to Ward 34, Derby City General Hospital. He indicates that he is not keen on taking any medication, but accepts the medication prescribed. He has problems sleeping and is prescribed Temazepam.

21 June 1995

Progress is such that AS is granted weekend leave by his rmo. He is not reported as hearing voices, and appears settled and prepared to continue taking medication. A provisional decision is made to discharge him towards the end of the month. AS states that he is reluctant to take oral medication, so depot medication is agreed and a test dose by depot injection is given on **28 June**. Due to concern expressed by AS on **28 June**, the planned discharge is changed to a period of leave, which is to end with AS's return to hospital on **6 July** for a second depot injection, after which, all being well, AS would be discharged.

6 July 1995

AS gives positive report of leave, is given injection and is discharged.

10 July 1995
The cpn rings AS at home. AS states he is willing to be visited but is very reluctant to have any further injections as he is aware of the nature of the medication and its side-effects and does not wish to continue with it.

13 July 1995
A discharge letter is written by a psychiatrist, who is not AS's rmo, to AS's GP. No mention is made of the collection of weapons by AS at the family home, or of potential family difficulties, or of his non-compliance with depot or oral medication. Follow-up arrangements include outpatient appointments with his rmo at Long Eaton clinic. AS's rmo later told the inquiry panel that she thought AS's father had agreed to keep an eye on his stepson's medication, but Mr (Peter) Smith has no recollection that he agreed to do this. Medication prescribed for AS on his discharge consists of depixol injections, fortnightly; sulpiride, twice daily, and procyclidine, as necessary. The inquiry panel considered that the medication prescribed conformed with good medical practice. The report comments, however, that serious risk indicators were not given their due weight, including emerging signs of non-compliance and an unhealthy interest in weapons. The report recommends that such information gathered from the community should be communicated to the multi-disciplinary team and to the clinical ward round.

19 July 1995
The cpn visits AS, taking the depot with him. AS seems relaxed, saying that the voices had lessened since taking sulpiride. The depot injection is, however, adamantly rejected. AS indicates that he is not willing to comply with the depot, and had discarded tablets in the past because they did not mix well with alcohol.

3 August 1995
The cpn visits AS again in an attempt to administer depot medication and to make a psychiatric assessment. There is a discussion of possible family problems. AS's mother indicates long-standing tension in their relationship. The cpn phones AS's rmo to report the situation. An appointment is made for AS and his mother to see the rmo at the Hospital on **23 August**.

8 August 1995
Anthony Smith kills his mother and half-brother by stabbing them to death in the family home. He uses a homemade weapon stored under his bed to beat his half-brother.

Note

The inquiry report is critical of the care provided because the poor communication between the professionals, which was adequate for routine business, lacked the necessary flexibility to deal with urgent or difficult cases. 'The system seemed to be weak and vacillating in dealing with a clear and potential danger, as was the refusal by Anthony Smith to accept his medication by injection....had he continued with his medication we have little doubt that there would have been no relapse and the tragedy would have been avoided'.

14 MARTIN MURSELL

The Report into the Care and Treatment of Martin Mursell
Lincoln Crawford QC, Manny Devaux, Dr Rob Ferris and Patricia Hayward
Published 7 March 1997 by Camden and Islington Health Authority, Hobson House, 155 Gower Street, London WC1E 6BH (0171 383 4155)

Summary

Martin Mursell was born in 1967. His mental illness began at about the age of 17 but was not diagnosed until his first admission to hospital four years later. In May 1988 he seriously assaulted his girlfriend. He was remanded in custody for four months and, in September 1988, sentenced to two months' imprisonment, suspended for one year, for actual bodily harm. His mother had wanted to take this opportunity to get him proper treatment and, accordingly, sought advice from her solicitor, whose response was, 'you don't want him locked up for life in a mental institution do you?'

In February 1989 he was admitted to hospital under s 2 of the Mental Health Act 1983 and then detained under s 3. He was given leave under s 17 at the end of March, which continued until he was discharged in July. He was subsequently admitted to hospital on three further occasions under s 3, from 18 January - 6 February 1990; 24 May - 17 September 1990 (on leave from 2 July), and from 18 January - 29 April 1993 (on leave from 8 April). He was admitted informally to hospital on 13 July 1994 and discharged on 3 August 1994.

In October 1994 Martin Mursell killed his step-father, Joseph Collins, aged 37, and attempted to kill his mother, Mary Collins. In January 1996, he pleaded guilty to murder and attempted murder and sentenced to life imprisonment and ten years' imprisonment, the sentences to run concurrently. He was subsequently transferred from prison to Rampton Hospital.

Medication

Martin Mursell had a history of non-compliance with medication in the community, non-attendance at outpatient appointments, and drug and alcohol misuse. MM and Mary Collins, his mother, often expressed concern at the high dosage levels of his medication, which was then reduced. This did not improve MM's compliance. His final admission to hospital was significant because he admitted himself and agreed to take oral medication (but not depot injections, which he regularly refused). His mother often noted the deterioration in his condition after periods of refusing medication but she was not always informed about the medication regime following her son's discharge from hospital.

Chronology

8 February 1989
MM's first admission to Whittington Hospital under s 2 MHA. He remains in hospital for two months. Staff do not gain any insight into his condition despite high doses of anti-psychotic medication.

23 March 1989
On leave of absence from Whittington, MM stops taking his medication. Although refusing to take depot injections he has a good rapport with his two community psychiatric nurses. He tells them

that the reason for his non-compliance is that high doses of oral chlorpromazine and haloperidol were too strong and made him feel like a 'zombie'.

26 April 1989
MM's carers plan to reduce his medication after his mother expresses concern at the high dosage. She is still concerned on **5 June**.

26 June-September 1989
MM attends ward round with his mother. He continues to be presecribed oral trifluoperazine. His mother is concerned by MM's deterioration and his failure to take the medication.

October 1989
The dosage of trifluoperazine is reduced, but MM's compliance remains poor and his condition deteriorates.

11 October 1989
MM takes an overdose of temazepam and trifluoperazine. He is taken to St. Bartholomew's Hospital and discharged the following day.

6 February 1990
MM is discharged from a section at Friern Hospital, having been admitted on **18 January**. He shows poor compliance in the community.

24 May 1990
He is admitted to Whittington Hospital under s 3 MHA and prescribed haloperidol orally. He refuses a depot injection.

25 June 1990
While in the Whittington on the section he agrees to depot injections.

3 November 1990
During the ward round to discuss his discharge MM gives an undertaking that he will accept depot injections of 500mg zuclopenthixol decanoate (clopixol) fortnightly from the cpn. MM and his mother attend the meeting where it is agreed that medication will be gradually reduced.

August 1991
The cpn who has been giving the depot injections stops working with MM. MM spends the next two and a half years in the community before his next admission. Initially, following his discharge from the Whittington, his contact with the cpn is good and his condition remains stable. However, when contact with the cpn ends he stops taking his medication.

29 January 1992
MM declines his mother's suggestion that he sees his rmo as an outpatient to discuss medication.

20 February 1992
MM is not taking medication prescribed and is becoming abusive and threatening.

4 March 1992
MM's mother sees his condition deteriorating due to his refusal to take medication.

21 January 1993
MM is transferred to Whittington Hospital from St Luke's. His medication is increased.

22 October 1993
MM runs out of medication. No information is given to his mother about MM's medication.

May 1993-1994
MM's compliance with medication is poor over the year. He suffers three oculogyric crises and is reluctant to take medication which produces 'dystonic side-effects', including a slight tremor in his legs. His dosage is reduced but compliance does not improve. MM seldom keeps outpatient appointments.

27 May 1994
MM informs his rmo that he has been using heroin for the past five years. He is unwilling to take any anti-psychotic medication.

13 July 1994
MM makes a voluntary admission to the Waterlow Unit at Whittington Hospital. His mother considers this to be a 'breakthrough' in her son's care. He refuses depot injections but agrees to take oral anti-psychotic medication.

3 August 1994
The discharge plan is for MM to continue to take his medication and this is to be monitored at outpatient appointments. He is encouraged to accept depot injections and social services are to find him accommodation. The cpn is to provide support to both MM and his mother.

28 October 1994
Martin Mursell kills Joe Collins and attempts to kill his mother, Mary Collins.

13 SUSAN PATRICIA JOUGHIN

Practice, Planning and Partnership: The Lessons to be learned from the Case of Susan Patricia Joughin
Alyson Leslie
Published 15 March 1997 by the Isle of Man Government, Department of Health (01624 642608)

Summary

Susan Joughin had an extensive and complex history of mental illness and had been admitted to hospital 14 times between 1980 and 1992. In February 1995, Susan Joughin, then aged 41, went to the police station and told them that she had injured her two daughters, aged seven and four. The younger child was pronounced dead on arrival at hospital but the older child survived. In March 1996 Susan Joughin pleaded guilty to manslaughter on the grounds of diminished responsibility and was made the subject of a hospital order with restrictions.

Medication

Much of the information about the role of medication in the care and treatment of Susan Joughin is contained in volume II of the inquiry report, the status of which has been declared by the Isle of Man authorities as confidential and which has not, therefore, been released to the general public.

It is known from the evidence that has been published that Susan Joughin (SJ) was extremely reluctant to take any medication and that she frequently failed to do so. In **August 1993** she received a prescription for two weeks' supply of medication and then missed seven consecutive appointments with her psychiatrist. This was not followed up, with the result that SJ did not see a psychiatrist for a total of twenty months. The community psychiatric nurse still had contact with SJ but did not know she was not receiving medication.

Note

The published volume of the inquiry report found that all the services responsible for the care of SJ failed jointly and individually to provide effective, quality care, especially in view of her non-compliance with medication. It was pointed out that when a patient subject to a care plan fails to attend two consecutive appointments, the responsible medical officer and the nominated keyworker should assess the situation and take appropriate action. Compulsory treatment under existing legislative powers should, the report stated, be given if the patient poses a risk to self or others.

The report's recommendations included introducing a system for keeping track of prescriptions issued to long-term patients so that if they are clearly going without medication the relevant medical practitioners are notified. Non-compliance in a patient should also trigger a review of the medication regime and its side-effects to determine whether these are discouraging compliance.

15 PAUL SMITH

Report of the Independent Panel of Inquiry into the Treatment and Care of Paul Smith
Jane Mishcon, Liam Hayes, Dr Michael Lowe and Michael Talbot
Published 9 July 1997 by North West Anglia Health Authority, St John's, Thorpe Rd, Peterborough PE3 6JG (01733 882288)

Summary

Paul Smith was born in 1966. His history of criminal behaviour began at the age of 13 with a conviction for criminal damage. Between the ages of 16 and 26 Paul Smith spent most of his time in youth custody or prison. Before he killed his mother's boyfriend, John McCluskey, in November 1995, his most serious offence was arson for which he received a 36 month jail term. Paul Smith had no contact with his local psychiatric services until five months after his release from prison, despite being assessed as a psychopath by the prison doctor of HMP Bedford. He was found guilty of the manslaughter of John McCluskey, on the grounds of diminished responsibility, and was made the subject of a hospital order with restrictions under ss 37/41 Mental Health Act 1983.

Medication

Paul Smith (PS) had a history of repeated absconsion from the ward while under section and continually discharged himself from hospital contrary to medical advice. Several examples of non-compliance are compounded by substance abuse.

Chronology

23 October 1992
PS is detained under s 3 MHA at the Edith Cavell Hospital. It is recorded in the nursing notes that it is not clear whether he is taking his prescribed anti-depressant medication. Doctors are asked to review the situation.

15 December 1992
On Ward 4 of Peterborough General Hospital PS refuses to go to the drugs trolley for medication during the night. He finally takes medication after 'persistent persuasion'.

3 March 1993
It is noted by a Doctor at the outpatient clinic that PS is no longer receiving depot injections but is still willing to take other forms of medication.

27 May 1993
During a domiciliary visit it is noted that PS is refusing depot medication and has not received an injection for over a month. He had also taken a recent overdose of his oral neuroleptic medication.

25 January 1994
At the review meeting with the rehabilitation team the occupational therapist technician's notes record PS' doctor asking him to take his medication as prescribed.

September 1994
PS fails to attend the rehabilitation unit throughout the month. A four week gap occurs in the administration of depot injections between **31 August** and **28 September**. PS' depot injections were planned to be administered fortnightly.

21 June 1995
The occupational therapist technician's notes record that PS is believed to be giving his medication away. The community psychiatric nurse is asked to look into this.

November 1995
Paul Smith kills John McCluskey

16 DORIS WALSH

Report of the Independent Inquiry into the Treatment and Care of Doris Walsh
Jane Mishcon, Lotte Mason, Shirley Stanner, Dr Donald Dick and Jane Mackay
Published 16 September 1997 by Coventry Health Authority, Christchurch House, Greyfriars Lane, Coventry CV1 2GQ (01203 552225)

Summary

In July 1995, Doris Walsh, aged 51, started a fire in her flat which led to the deaths of her neighbour Tom Redshaw and his son, Richard, aged 13. Her first contact with psychiatric services was in 1975, after an overdose of anti-depressants. She had been suffering from episodes of depression since the birth of her daughter but had not sought any professional help until the mid 1970s. Between August 1986 and July 1996 Doris Walsh was admitted to Walsgrave Hospital on six occasions for treatment of her depression. On 9 July 1995 she failed to return to Walsgrave from weekend leave and subsequently told social workers from the community mental health team that she was unwilling to return to hospital. On 7 October 1996 Doris Walsh was found not guilty of manslaughter of Tom and Richard Redshaw by reason of insanity. Since her trial she has been detained under a Hospital Order with restrictions, ss 37/41 of the Mental Health Act 1983.

Medication

Doris Walsh (DW) had a psychiatric history dating back twenty years. She had had thirteen nervous breakdowns and received various diagnoses on several different occasions. At the time of the homicides, she had been a voluntary patient receiving treatment for depression at Walsgrave Hospital's psychiatric unit, but had discharged herself to live in Alpha House block of flats in Coventry, just seventeen days prior to the deaths.

Chronology

September 1982
DW has not been taking medication for a few months but is seen by a GP who restarts her prescription. The psychiatrist who had seen her on **4 March** had told her to continue with mianserin for two to four months, and duphaston for about a year.

18 July 1989
DW is admitted informally to Walsgrave Hospital. She has been feeling low for four weeks previously. She feels her husband and daughter are turning against her. It emerges that one week prior to the onset of these symptoms she had stopped taking the stelazine prescribed.

15 January 1991
At an outpatient review DW reports she is feeling depressed. She had reduced her own medication from 200mg prothiaden to 100mg before Christmas and has also reported that she is not sleeping and has a poor appetite. It is felt the pattern for relapse is re-emerging.

4 June 1991
Having been admitted to hospital on an informal basis in **March** for ECT, and having gone missing on her return home in **April**, her psychiatrist writes to her GP in the following terms: 'Doris Walsh

left her residence.... she had been irregular with her medication... [T]hough she takes dothiepin (in an inadequate dose), she had stopped taking the other drugs, including lithium'.

21 July 1992
DW attends her GP's surgery (now in Leamington Spa) after she has been in the A&E department of Warwick Hospital following a panic attack. DW's partner tells her GP that she has attempted suicide in the past few days, and DW tells the GP that she should be on lithium but has not been taking it because it makes her feel 'knocked out'.

August 1992
At the end of the month her GP notes that DW has reduced her dothiepin/prothiaden dose because she dislikes sedation. She is advised to take the full dose.

30 April 1993
The day after moving into Alpha House flats in Coventry, DW turns up at the outpatient clinic at Walsgrave Hospital feeling very depressed. She tells staff she has not been taking lithium for the past two months and has been feeling particularly bad during the last two weeks.

June 1995
DW is admitted to Walsgrave Hospital A&E with a cut ankle and reports hearing voices for the past year. She also indicates that she has not been taking her medication. DW is admitted to the psychiatric wing as a voluntary patient.

11 July 1995
An approved social worker visits DW at Alpha House because she has not returned to Walsgrave Hospital where she is a voluntary patient. DW tells the asw she has not taken any medication recently and does not have any, but says she will visit her GP in the afternoon to get some. Although she does attend, it is unclear if she actually collects her prescription.

28 July 1995
Doris Walsh sets fire to her cupboard in her flat to combat the voices she hears coming from it with the result that her neighbours Tom Redshaw, and his son Richard, die from the effects of smoke inhalation.

17 SARAH BEYNON

Summary of the Report of the Inquiry into the Treatment and Care of Ms B
Bridgit Dimond, Dr Paul Bowden, David Sallah, Roy Holden and Richard Lingham
Published 15 October 1997 by Avon Health Authority, 10 Dighton Street, Bristol BS2 8EE (0117 9002 400)

Summary

In May 1994 Sarah Beynon began to develop symptoms of mental illness and was referred by her GP to psychiatric services. She had a long history of substance abuse and there was a family history of mental disorder. On 25 August 1994 she was admitted to Southmead Hospital under s 2 of the Mental Health Act 1983, followed by a s 3 admission in September 1994. She was subsequently transferred to the Fromeside Regional Secure Unit. While on s 17 leave Sarah Beynon killed her father, in August 1995. At Bristol Crown Court she pleaded guilty to manslaughter on the grounds of diminished responsibility and was made the subject of a hospital order with restrictions (ss 37/41 MHA) and admitted to Broadmoor Hospital.

Medication

Sarah Beynon (SB) was referred to the psychiatric services by her GP for the treatment of schizophrenia/psychosis. She was admitted to Southmead Hospital and later transferred to Fromeside Regional Secure Unit (rsu). She developed paranoid ideas preceded by beliefs that her father had sexually abused her. Staff treated these claims as evidence of her illness in conjunction with a long history of substance abuse and a family history of mental disorder. It is considered unusual for a patient with a first episode of psychosis to be sent to a regional secure unit. SB regularly absconded from care. Section 117 planning was not used during periods of leave and Frenchay Healthcare NHS Trust did not implement the care programme approach in defining and delivering the patient's aftercare needs.

Chronology

25 August 1994
SB admitted under s 2 to Southmead Hospital

21 September 1994
Section 3 admission to Southmead Hospital There is a failure to draw up and implement a management plan. Compliance with medication is not achieved. When it is, the full dose ranges are not given with the result that SB's psychosis is not controlled. The report states that the ward did not have the necessary resources to contain a patient like SB with these challenges. There was no consistency in administering depot neuroleptic medication and medication given for leave periods may not have been taken. There was, additionally, a failure to follow up the possibility that SB's psychosis was drug induced

9 March 1995
Transfer to Fromeside Clinic. Following admission SB's medication is increased over a six week period before the control of her psychosis is achieved. No drug screening takes place at Fromeside at any time and neither is there any formal assessment of risk.

July 1995
Clear evidence that SB is controlling contact with staff.

July-August 1995
SB effectively an outpatient due to absconsions following s.17 leave. Section 117 meeting is planned for **6 September**.

August 1995
Reduction of medication takes place but SB is not being closely monitored. Decision made to reduce medication is not taken by the rmo, who is on leave, but by the senior registrar, as is the decision to grant extended leave.

30 August 1995
Sarah Beynon kills her Father.

18 DAMIAN WITTS

Inquiry into the Treatment and Care of Damian Witts
Richard Lingham and Dr Julian Candy
Published 10 December 1997 by Gloucestershire Health Authority, Victoria Warehouse, The Docks, Gloucester GL1 2EL (01452 300222)

Summary

On 26 September 1995, within hours of returning from Coleford House Day Hospital, Damian Witts, a diagnosed schizophrenic, had stabbed his brother John to death. His keyworker, in January 1995, had suggested an alternative diagnosis to schizophrenia. The alternative diagnosis, which attributed the symptoms manifested by the patient to 'flashbacks or past experiences', was not subjected to a full multidisciplinary review. Damian Witts assumed the possibility of an alternative diagnosis made it unnecessary to take his medication. The notes of his hospital visit on 20 September 1995 show that he was using illicit drugs, neglecting himself and not taking his medication. In July 1996 Damian Witts pleaded guilty to manslaughter on the grounds of diminished responsibility and was made the subject of a hospital order with restrictions under ss 37/41 of the Mental Health Act 1983.

Medication

The initial diagnosis made in May/June 1991 was schizophrenia. Damian Witts' keyworker suggested a possible alternative diagnosis, in May 1995, of post traumatic stress disorder (this was not subject to multidisciplinary review). There was a failure to review DW's care programme, particularly in 1995. From June 1993 DW attended Coleford House Day Hospital (Severn NHS Trust) each week as an outpatient. There was evidence of long-standing misuse of both prescribed and illicit drugs.

Chronology

Early 1995
Having been diagnosed with schizophrenia in August 1991, and prescribed medication, DW attends day hospital. His medication is supervised by his girlfriend. DW is regularly using illicit drugs but there is inadequate drug screening within Severn NHS Trust.

26 July 1995
The cpa review makes no mention of medication compliance.

26 August 1995
DW's girlfriend leaves their home and without her supervision DW fails to take his medication. DW increases his abuse of illicit drugs.

20 September 1995
The record of DW's hospital visit highlights non-compliance with medication.

26 September 1995
Damian Witts kills his brother John Witts.

19 NORMAN DUNN

Report of the Independent Inquiry into the Treatment and Care of Norman Dunn
David Keating, Dr Paul Collins and Sandra Walmsley
Published 16 December 1997 by Newcastle and North Tyneside Health Authority, Benfield Road, Newcastle upon Tyne NE6 4PF (0191 219 6064)

Summary

Norman Dunn developed schizophrenia in 1968. He was in regular contact with local mental health services predominantly as an outpatient but had several admissions as an inpatient when his condition deteriorated. He lived alone after his divorce in 1984 and his mother became his primary carer. His relationship with his family was a difficult one, particularly with his mother, whom he accused of stealing from him. It was after another argument over money that he killed her in July 1995. Although Norman Dunn had received much of his care in the community the independent inquiry found that there had been a failure adequately to assess his ability to care for himself and a relapse could easily have been predicted. Norman Dunn was convicted in June 1996 of the manslaughter of his mother on the grounds of diminished responsibility, and was made the subject of a hospital order with restrictions under ss 37/41 of the Mental Health Act 1983.

Medication

Norman Dunn (ND) regularly attended the local day centre and he was given much of his depot medication at the clinic. He was an alcoholic. ND believed his mother was cheating him out of money, that his food and drink were being poisoned and that his flat was bugged. With some pressure from him, his medication was substantially reduced and there was evidence of non-compliance in the period leading to the killing of his mother.

Chronology

11 August 1971
ND's condition deteriorates and depot injections of modecate (fluphenazine decanoate) commence.

22 October 1983
He is admitted to St George's Hospital under s 2 MHA following an overdose of benzhexol. He is discharged on **7 January 1984**.

2 March 1993
After admission to the North Tyneside General Hospital (NTGH), it is discovered that ND has not been taking his prescribed medication since **24 February** (the discharge date of his previous admission to NTGH).

6 April 1993
ND is detained under s 3 at NTGH. He is discharged on **10 September 1993**. At the time of this discharge his medication is 150mg flupenthixol weekly, 5mg procyclidine four times a day, 15mg trifluoperazine three times a day, 40mg fluoxetine daily and two senna at night.

8 October 1993
ND receives his weekly injection at the depot clinic of 150mg flupenthixol. He continues to attend on a regular basis.

1 March 1994
At the request of ND, his medication is reviewed at an outpatient clinic with his rmo. Oral medication is discontinued and is to be reviewed in one month's time. Procyclidine is continued to be prescribed.

14 March 1994
At the s 117 meeting, ND complains of experiencing the 'jitters' (seeing flashing lights and hearing voices) as a result, he claims, of reducing his drinking to two pints per session. It is decided his rmo is to review the medication regime, following concern expressed by the cpn who had picked up 'trigger words' in conversation with ND.

12 April 1994
The rmo reduces the dose of procyclidine to 5mg once a day.

22 April 1994
The injections ND is receiving at the depot clinic are reduced from 150 mg flupenthixol once a week to once every two weeks. This reduces the dosage by half and reduces the contact ND has with depot clinic staff, with whom he would normally raise any concerns he had about medication and how he felt in general.

13 June 1994
At the s 117 meeting ND complains of the side-effects of the depot injections. He also states that he is consuming only small amounts of alcohol. It is decided that the rmo is to review medication.

17 June 1994
The dosage of flupenthixol is reduced from 150 mg to 100 mg.

15 July 1994
The dosage of flupenthixol is reduced to 60 mg and administered every four weeks.

1 August 1994
The keyworker (cpn) visits ND who complains that the depot injections are unnecessary and describes hearing 'voices in his head' that can last for hours and disturb his sleep. The keyworker notes ND's alcohol intake of up to four or five pints daily. ND claims his drinks are being 'spiked'. The keyworker feels no further action is warranted and expects to see ND at the s 117 meeting on **26 September**.

26 September 1994
At the s 117 review meeting it is decided that ND is coping with minimal support and is to be discharged from the s 117 register. The care plan needs are monitoring of medication and ensuring ND receives medication as necessary. Mrs MacLachlan says ND is 'not himself' and ND says that he feels better on lithium carbonate.

4 October 1994
The rmo considers increasing the dose of ND's depot medication because his 'symptoms were starting to break through again'. ND is against any increase so it is kept at the current level.

30 November 1994
ND sees a locum consultant psychiatrist. Medication is continued as before.

March 1995
ND has one of his regular meetings with his son, who is shocked at his sudden deterioration. His son estimates that ND is drinking between six and eight pints per day. ND is referring to Mrs MacLachlan at this time as 'the devil'. Other family members remark on ND's increasingly strange behaviour.

31 May 1995
During an outpatient visit ND is seen by another doctor who reduces the dosage of the depot injection to 20mg flupenthixol administered fortnightly. He also notes ND's drinking has increased to five to six pints per day and warns him that any further increase will counteract the benefits of the depot.

30 June 1995
ND attends the depot clinic without his medication (this is prescribed by the doctor and collected by the patient). He tells staff he is 'all right' and does not want any more depot injections. No medication is kept at the clinic and ND leaves without receiving his injection. ND's key worker is not alerted. Staff intend to raise the matter at the team meeting on **4 July**.

1 July 1995
Norman Dunn kills his mother, Eileen MacLachlan.

20 DESMOND LEDGESTER

'Sharing the Burden.' An Independent Inquiry into the Care and Treatment of Desmond Ledgester
V J Double, Peter McGinnis, Terry Nelson and Jeremy Pritlove
Published 12 January 1998 by Calderdale & Kirklees Health Authority, St. Lukes House, Blackmoorfoot Road, Huddersfield, West Yorkshire HD4 5RH (01484 466000)

Summary

Desmond Ledgester first had contact with mental health services in December 1993. Diagnosed as suffering from schizophrenia, he received treatment as an outpatient and as a voluntary inpatient on Ward F of Halifax General Hospital. Between June and August 1994 he was receiving treatment at a health centre until he failed to attend his fortnightly appointments. The community psychiatric nurse felt this was a sign that Desmond Ledgester no longer wanted contact with psychiatric services. In December 1994 he was admitted to Halifax Royal Infirmary after taking an overdose of paracetamol. His contact with psychiatric services resumed in March 1995 when he was again admitted to Ward F. While absent without leave from the Hospital, on 24 March 1995, Ledgester was discharged. He was arrested on the 6 July 1995 and charged with the murder of Malcolm Hodgeson in the early hours of Wednesday 21 June. It was determined that Ledgester was unfit to plead and he was transferred to Rampton Hospital under ss 48/49 of the Mental Health Act 1983.

Chronology

16 December 1993
DL is referred by his GP to a consultant psychiatrist who diagnoses schizophrenia. The consultant psychiatrist prescribes 1mg risperidone, increasing to 3 mg twice daily. Medical notes show DL has worries about the side effects of the medication. DL regularly attends the outpatient clinic.

30 December 1993
Medical notes from the outpatient clinic show DL's compliance is 'not good' and he is having trouble sleeping. He is prescribed 3mg risperidone twice daily and 7.5mg zimovane at night.

20 January 1994
At the outpatient clinic DL is prescribed four weeks' supply of risperidone and zimovane. The prescribing doctor notes that he becomes paranoid easily.

17 March 1994
DL requests changes to his medication. Not only is the current medication regime maintained but, in addition, 5mg procyclidine when necessary and 50mg thioridazine when required for insomnia, are also prescribed.

14 April 1994
At the outpatient clinic DL complains he is not eating or sleeping properly and requests temazepam. This is refused. The dose of thioridazine is increased to 75 mg at night.

4 May 1994
The rmo writes to DL's cpn and says that the risperidone has made little difference and his thioridazine has been increased.

7 May 1994
Two cpns visit DL at home to make an assessment of him. He complains that his medication does not seem to help and it is suggested that he receive depixol injections. DL tells them that in the past he has used LSD, ecstasy and marijuana. He is allocated a new cpn.

16 May 1994
At the outpatient clinic DL's medication is changed to 20mg paroxetine daily.

27 May 1994
DL is given depixol. The initial dose is 10 mg followed by depot injections of 20 mg every two weeks given by his cpn at the health centre. The prescription of paroxetine continues.

7 June 1994
During a visit by his cpn, DL is advised of side-effects of depixol and how to deal with any residual symptoms that the depot injections fail to suppress.

June 1994 -August 1994
The cpn continues to give DL his depot injections but irregularly, due to DL missing appointments. The cpn makes efforts to find DL whenever he does not attend.

August 1994
DL receives his last depot injection. The cpn makes several visits to his home but he is never there at the time of the visit. He does see DL 'around Halifax' but is never close enough to speak to him. The cpn states that on these occasions DL did not seem overtly ill. He feels that DL is now misusing drugs and that this is the cause of his failure to attend the health centre. DL had admitted to the cpn he was having 'one smoke a day'.

6 September 1994
The cpn writes to DL's rmo and GP advising them he is no longer in contact with him and that he believes DL no longer wishes to continue treatment and that he must respect DL's 'decision'.

11 December 1994
DL is taken by his mother to the Royal Halifax Infirmary after an overdose of 25 paracetamol tablets. He admits not taking his prescribed medication saying he felt it did not work. He is seen as aggressive, distressed and suicidal. After being administered ipecacuanha he is admitted to the ward.

12 December 1994
DL discharges himself having agreed to see the psychiatrist. An appointment is made for him and notification of it sent in the post. DL does not attend the appointment and no effort is made to contact him further.

10 March 1995
DL's GP sees a member of his family and arranges for himself or a cpn to visit DL to recommend depot injections or being sectioned under the Mental Health Act 1983. The GP's feeling is that DL has stopped receiving his depot injections.

15 March 1995
DL is admitted to ward F of Halifax General Hospital after being arrested. The admitting doctor records in his notes that his impressions are, 'drug induced schizophrenia'. He prescribes 75mg chlorpromazine. DL is allowed to visit his flat the next day but returns to hospital that evening.

17 March 1995
DL refuses to take his medication during the morning rounds. He agrees to take his medication at 5 pm and 10 pm. At 1.15 am he is given 7.5mg zopiclone to help him sleep.

20 March 1995
Ward round notes by staff are contradictory. Some record that DL is not present. However, the staff nurse records in his notes, 'Prescribed Clopixol depot 100 mg, Clopixol 20 mg orally on day one, 20 mg TDS after: Clopixol acuphase 150 mg I/M Lorezapam 4 mg if he will take it'.

21 March 1995
DL declines medication.

22 March 1995
DL leaves the ward.

23 March 1995
The rmo notes that DL is to be reviewed for possible section if he returns to the ward. Another doctor records that if DL has not returned by 5 pm he will be discharged in his absence.

24 March 1995
DL discharged in his absence.

3 April 1995
DL goes to see his GP but sees a locum. DL tells him that he is using drugs.

7 April 1995
DL is re-admitted to ward F of Halifax General Hospital but leaves with his family after two to three hours. A decision is made to discharge him in his absence if he does not return.

21 June 1995
Desmond Ledgester is arrested for the murder of Malcolm Hodgeson.

CHAPTER FIVE

NON-COMPLIANCE AND THE INDEPENDENT INQUIRIES ANALYSIS AND DISCUSSION

Analysis

Following the details of the inquiries set out in the previous chapter, it is now possible to take a further look at them and to analyse in a little more detail those factors in particular which were found to influence non-compliance, and to express them as a total and percentage of the 20 cases out of the 35 studied in total in which non-compliance was a major contributory factor. Clearly 20 cases represent a small sample but issues of interest are raised from this sample which need to be addressed in future policy developments which have, as part of their task, the responsibility of providing effective and comprehensive services to those who are among the most difficult patients to engage in the community.

Factor in non-compliance	Number of cases (out of 20)	
• lack of insight	16	(80%)
• non-attendance	10	(50%)
• staff-patient relationship	4	(20%)
• side-effects (incl.refusal of depot injections)	17	(85%)
• substance abuse	13	(65%)
• poor information-sharing	9	(45%)
• poor communication with family/patient	11	(55%)
• poor aftercare and supervision	17	(85%)

As the inquiries set out in the previous chapter clearly demonstrate, non-compliance with medication does not only result in the reduced efficacy of therapeutic drugs. It can also lead to a relapse in the condition, the need for additional treatment and thus readmission to hospital (the 'revolving door' patient). For the majority of patients, readmission to hospital needs to be avoided if at all possible, as it leads to a gradual deterioration in the patient's condition, as well as a drain on resources. The preferred option for care is for patients to live in the community with friends and family. In the inquiry reports studied by The Zito Trust, however, it is clear there are numerous obstacles to achieving this desired objective. Patients suffering from mental illness often lack insight into the nature of their condition and this diminishes their understanding of the need for medication or other treatment, particularly when they start feeling well again as a direct result of the medicine they have been using.

A major cause of non-compliance among the mentally ill is the often high side-effect profile of the conventional type of medication used to treat more serious mental illnesses such as schizophrenia and manic depression. These side-effects can be serious and disabling, as they affect the autonomic nervous system which acts upon the body but which is not under conscious control. Side-effects include dry mouth, blurred vision and increased sweating. There can also be an interruption of sexual function and a feeling of great lethargy.

Additionally, there are the side-effects known as extrapyramidal symptoms (EPS, so called because they affect the extrapyramidal motor tract in the brain). These symptoms are the most problematic and are similar to those seen in Parkinson's disease. They range from muscular rigidity, eye-rolling, trembling, uncontrollable tic-like movements (tardive dyskinesia) and an inner restlessness known as akathisia. These side-effects are not present in everybody taking this type of medication and can vary in severity between individuals. It is clear, however, that the awareness and experience of such side-effects can have a dramatic impact on any individual, particularly if he or she is required to take medication on a daily basis.

There are, therefore, serious quality of life implications for patients who take antipsychotic medication, especially when it is the case that they may have to take it for an indefinite period of time. It is perhaps not surprising then that patients often cease taking their medication mainly due to side-effects, particularly when they no longer feel any symptoms of their mental illness. The inquiry reports show how often this is the principal reason expressed by the patient.

Discussion

Lack of insight

Lack of insight or a refusal to accept a diagnosis of mental illness is a major factor in most of the cases of non-compliance and is also a factor in those cases where non-compliance was not itself a factor. Much has been written about lack of insight and its negative impact on the provision of care and patient compliance with treatment. Plainly, if someone does not consider themselves to be mentally ill, they are unlikely to accept a care package and comply with medication. Of the 20 cases in which non-compliance with medication was an factor, only in one case, that of Richard Burton, was lack of insight *not* an obvious issue.

It is useful to note that those patients who are of above-average intelligence show considerable resourcefulness in controlling the terms of their own treatment. They also appear to be adept in disguising or misreporting their non-compliance, which must be viewed in the context of their lack of insight and readiness to withdraw from treatment plans when they show signs of improvement. Frank Hampshire, for example, was found to have dictated the terms of his own treatment, in large part by dissimulating the extent and severity of his illness and his non-compliance. Insight can have a powerfully positive impact on compliance. Martin Mursell, who lacked insight throughout most of his illness, gained insight shortly before the index offence by admitting himself to hospital. This insight was accompanied by his agreeing to take oral antipsychotic medication, having been non-compliant throughout the course of his illness. Other factors, however, namely his discharge, poor aftercare, inevitable non-compliance and drug-abuse negated this positive development.
Reports: CC AR PM SL KG JM NG FH MM SJ PS DWalsh SB DWitts ND DL

Non-attendance

Non-attendance at outpatient appointments or day hospital, or a failure to attend appointments made by and with members of the psychiatric team and/or social services is characteristic of patients who are considered difficult to manage, who regularly reject

aftercare in the community on discharge from hospital, or whose mental health has deteriorated to such an extent that non-attendance is inevitable. Non-attendance, rather than acting as a trigger for more engaged or pro-active care by members of the psychiatric and social services, is rarely followed up. Indeed, in some cases, such as that of Michael Buchanan, non-attendance results in the patient being dropped from the community psychiatric nurse's caseload and so losing contact with psychiatric services. Non-attendance is a factor in most of the cases resulting in homicide, but was found to be a factor in non-compliance in 10 of the 20 cases.
Reports: CC MB FH RB MM SJ PS DWalsh SB DL

Relationship with professional carers

The personal relationship between patient and carer is of considerable importance in achieving and maintaining compliance. While a good relationship will not guarantee compliance, a bad one virtually guarantees non-compliance. Equally, a good and trusting relationship which then breaks down or is terminated is likely to lead to non-compliance with the medication regime. This is a factor in any system of community care. Another factor identified in research, which is directly related to the carer-patient relationship, is the level of patient involvement in decision-making. The 'barely adequate' section 117 aftercare planning meeting attended by Stephen Laudat, combined with his dislike of his responsible medical officer, made compliance in the community extremely unlikely. Similarly, the failure in February 1991 to arrange a review of Christopher Clunis' medication regime, *at his request*, led directly to his non-compliance. A patient's personal dislike of his/her cpn or rmo was a significant factor in only one of the reports in which non-compliance was a major issue. In a further two, the ending of a trusting relationship with a member of the community psychiatric services led to a deterioration in compliance with the treatment regimes.
Reports: CC SL MM SB

Side-effects, the prescribed dose and depot injections

The adverse side-effects of anti-psychotic medication or a disagreement with medical staff over the dose prescribed, leads to non-compliance in the majority of cases in which non-compliance is an issue. Similarly, a failure to review medication on a regular basis in conjunction with the patient and the keyworker or cpn leads to a deterioration in compliance. A further factor cited in the Royal Pharmaceutical Society report, discussed in chapter two, as contributing to this is the actual strength of the dose of medication given and the frequency with which it needs to be taken - as each increases, compliance decreases. The evidence on this matter from the present research is ambiguous. Andrew Robinson refused to accept the normal dose of medication in the year leading up to the homicide, despite the dose being very near to the lowest acceptable level, but was for a short time compliant with a half dose before refusing all medication. In the case of Martin Mursell, however, a reduction in the dose did not increase compliance.

Non-compliance due to adverse side-effects is in some cases due to research by the patient into the side-effects of medication, both possible and experienced, or can be due to a dislike of one particular side-effect, for example, in the case of Stephen Laudat, impotence. Again, failure in communication can lead to non-compliance - where a doctor fails to inform the patient of the range of possible side effects a drug may cause, or the alternative treatments available, the patient may not wish to continue with their medication and simply stop, whereas if there had been greater communication they might have asked for a different regime. Non-compliance due to adverse side-effects or disagreement with the prescribed dose is a factor in 13 of the 20 cases.
Reports: CC AR JR SL JM NG FH AS MM SJ DWitts ND DL

In a number of cases, patient dislike of depot injections was highlighted as a problem in achieving compliance. These patients often accept oral medication instead of depot injections. However, due to the difficulty of monitoring oral medication, compliance becomes difficult to assess. The refusal of depot injections was a factor in four cases.
Refusal of injections: NG MM PS ND

Substance abuse

The interaction between substance abuse and non-compliance is complex. Abuse of alcohol or drugs leads to an increase in non-compliance, in part because drugs and alcohol produce adverse side-effects when mixed with antipsychotic medication. Drug and alcohol abuse also impacts negatively on compliance as it leads to a deterioration of the patient's mental health, which in turn may increase non-compliance. Crime associated with the need to finance a drug or alcohol problem, which may in part be a result of non-compliance, may indirectly lead to a temporary increase in compliance as a patient is brought, sometimes via the police service or criminal justice system, into contact with the psychiatric services. The improvement in compliance and consequent improvement in mental health is often temporary as the patient becomes a victim of the 'revolving door' cycle of community care.

A more substantial piece of research on substance abuse, mental illness and homicide was published in February 1998 by Alcohol Concern (Ward and Applin, 1998). The research looked at 17 homicide reports and found that drink and drugs played a major part in 14 of them. In the majority of these 14 cases, the killer had an identifiable substance misuse problem. The report goes on to warn that all too often the authorities fail to tackle drink and drug problems which, when combined with mental illness, can be a major contributory factor in the circumstances leading to homicide (and even more so to suicide and self-harm).

Substance abuse *and non-compliance* was a factor in 13 of The Zito Trust's 20 non-compliance cases.
Reports: MB JR PM KG JM AS MM PS DWalsh SB DWitts ND DL

Poor information-sharing or communication

Poor inter-agency and intra-agency information-sharing on non-compliance is a factor in nine of the 20 cases in which non-compliance is a factor. One or a number of members of a team may have knowledge about the patient's compliance with medication, but that information is either not widely disseminated or is not passed on to the clinical staff in a

consistent or systematic manner. In the case of Christopher Clunis, a report prepared for court by two psychiatrists was not in the hands of a third psychiatrist who discharged Clunis from Guy's Hospital a month later in September 1992, believing Clunis to be 'completely well'. The report prepared for the court in August read: 'Although his psychosis is coming under control with medication he shows little insight into the need for continuing treatment. He would not cooperate with treatment outside the hospital and would be likely to relapse. He could again act in a dangerous way if he becomes floridly psychotic'.
Reports: CC NG FH AS MM SJ DWalsh SB DWitts

Note: In addition, differences in diagnosis between psychiatrists may lead to changing medication regimes, in which the patient is prescribed medication or has it withdrawn, depending on the psychiatrist. This pattern is evident in the Andrew Robinson and Jason Mitchell reports.

Poor communication on compliance with family and patient

In a number of cases vital information on compliance was known to the family of the patient, but was either not communicated to the services, or was communicated but not acted upon by social or psychiatric services. Failure to communicate fully with the family may result in undue weight being given to the reports of compliance given by the patient himself, who in the majority of cases examined, lacked insight into his condition. Andrew Robinson's parents contacted the psychiatric and social services on numerous occasions, informing them of their son's non-compliance and deterioration. The inquiry report comments: 'The overwhelming impression they gained was that professionals paid more attention to their own brief interviews with Andrew than they did to family and friends who were in daily contact with him'. Poor communication about compliance with the patient and/or his family was a factor in 11 of the 20 cases.
Reports: AR PM SL NG FH AS MM SJ PS DWalsh ND

Poor aftercare and supervision

Closely related to the failings highlighted above, the failure of psychiatric and social services to address non-compliance in the community is, not surprisingly, evident in the majority of cases in which non-compliance is a factor. Of the 20 cases, poor follow-up is a factor in 17 of them. Poor follow-up takes many forms. It may involve some or all of the factors examined in 'poor information-sharing' or 'poor communication on compliance with family and patient', and in addition involve failure to follow-up non-attendance, or even discharging a patient from a caseload as a result of non-attendance or absconsion, as happened in the cases of Buchanan and Grey. Or it may involve the cancellation of appointments with the patient by clinical staff (as happened in the case of John Rous). It may also involve an inadequate aftercare package and/or inadequate monitoring and reviewing of the effectiveness of the aftercare plan. A lack of pro-active engagement may involve an over-ready acceptance of non-compliance which may be combined with a failure to recognise and closely monitor the effects of accepting non-compliance (as happened in the case of Stephen Laudat).

Unsurprisingly, all nine cases of poor information-sharing in or between mental health services also showed poor follow-up, while nine of the 11 cases of poor communication about compliance with the family or patient also showed poor follow-up practices. Plainly, from this evidence, adequate follow-up in the community cannot be provided without communication among professional carers and between professional and informal carers and the patient and the patient's family.
Reports: CC MB AR JR SL KG JM NG FH AS MM SJ DWalsh SB DWitts ND DL

Comment

Most of the inquiry reports refrain from speculating as to the possible outcomes had the non-compliant patient in question adhered to the treatment regime prescribed. The Gadher Report, however, is more specific and concludes: '[t]his tragedy probably occurred because NG was out of hospital and driving a car at a time when he was not taking the medication which he needed and was unwell.....[a]lthough it was, we think, predictable that he would stop taking oral medication and that he might, in consequence, become unwell, and that if unwell he might exhibit some degree of violence, we do not consider that a tragedy of this magnitude was predictable.' The report makes a causal link between Gadher's release, his non-compliance, his relapse and his propensity for violence. The tragedy was not predictable, but it was preventable. The report further concludes that the failure to foster compliance was due to the reliance by carers on a failed management plan and on their failure to consider and implement a more assertive plan.

In the case of Anthony Smith, the report concludes that, 'had he continued with his medication we have little doubt that there would have been no relapse and the tragedy would have been avoided.' The report further criticises the system of communication between professionals, which was adequate for routine matters, but lacked the flexibility to deal with urgent or difficult cases. 'The system seemed to be weak and vacillating in dealing with a clear and potential danger, as was the refusal by AS to accept his medication by injection.'

The Gadher report contains two recommendations on clinical practice, made in view of the reliance by the psychiatric team on a failed management plan. The report recommends, 'that outpatient reviews of patients subject to the [care programme approach] procedure should be under the close supervision of the responsible consultant. We further recommend that doctors without the qualification MRCPsych should not assess patients except under supervision.' The Anthony Smith report, responding to the failure to respond to warning signs of non-compliance, recommends that such information should be communicated to the multidisciplinary and clinical team on the ward round.

The Joughin and Mursell reports both produce recommendations relating to the need to review the medication regime when non-compliance occurs. The Mursell report recommends, 'that where there is evidence of poor or non-compliance with treatment or persistent failure to keep out-patient appointments, the key worker should bring this to the attention of the multi-disciplinary team who devised the original plan, and a clear strategy worked out to try and improve compliance.' The Joughin report produces a number of recommendations on non-compliance. Echoing the Mursell report (published in the same month), the report recommends that, 'non-compliance with medication should trigger a review of the medication regime and of any possible side effects, to determine whether these are discouraging compliance.' Responding to the poor level of communication between clinical and multidisciplinary teams and patients and carers, the report recommends that, '[p]atients and carers should be given information about their medication and have the reasons for changes in medication explained to them', and that, '[t]reatment regimes should aim to achieve the maximum effect for the minimum level of medication. Medication should be reviewed regularly and customised to the response of the patient.' The report also proposes a system for tracking prescriptions: 'A system must be in place for keeping track of what prescriptions have been issued to long-term patients and of alerting the relevant medical practitioners when patients have clearly run out of medication but have not received a recent prescription. In such instances a prescription should not simply be sent out to the patient without their being seen.'

Many other recommendations from these and other reports, particularly in relation to communication, inter-agency working and note keeping and storage, are also relevant to the issue of non-compliance with medication and their implementation would do much to improve compliance.

Reference

Ward, M. and Applin, C. (1998) *The Unlearned Lesson: The Role of Alcohol and Drug Misuse in Homicides Perpetrated by People with Mental Health Problems*. London: Wynne Howard Books.

CHAPTER SIX

HOMICIDE BY PEOPLE WITH MENTAL ILLNESS
A SUMMARY OF CURRENT STATISTICS FROM THE HOME OFFICE AND THE NATIONAL CONFIDENTIAL INQUIRY

This chapter sets out to summarise the statistics regarding homicide committed by people with mental illness. The statistics and information are taken from four Home Office publications, and the progress report published by the Director of the National Confidential Inquiry into Suicide and Homicide by People with Mental Illness, published in December 1997. All five publications are fully referenced at the end of the chapter:

(a) Home Office Criminal Statistics: England and Wales 1996
(b) Home Office Statistical Bulletin: Statistics of Mentally Disordered Offenders 1996
(c) Home Office Statistical Bulletin: Statistics of Mentally Disordered Offenders 1995
(d) Home Office Statistical Bulletin: Statistics of Mentally Disordered Offenders 1994
(e) The National Confidential Inquiry into Suicide and Homicide by People with Mental Illness (Progress Report)

The conclusions which we reach from the following analysis of Home Office statistics have been agreed with by the Home Office Research and Statistics Directorate, and we are grateful for the Directorate's examination of our work.

In order to provide some context, Table 1 below shows the total number of offences currently recorded as homicide for the years 1982-1996.

<u>TABLE 1: TOTAL NUMBER OF OFFENCES CURRENTLY RECORDED AS HOMICIDE</u> (ref. (a), p84)

Current homicides	*1982*	*1983*	*1984*	*1985*	*1986*	*1987*	*1988*	*1989*	*1990*	*1991*	*1992*	*1993*	*1994*	*1995*	*1996*
Number	557	482	537	536	563	599	547	524	555	623	581	566	635	663	627
Per million population	11.2	9.7	10.8	10.7	11.2	11.9	10.9	10.4	10.9	12.2	11.3	11.0	12.3	12.8	12.1

'Homicide' includes the offences of murder, manslaughter and infanticide. Since deaths may be initially recorded as homicide but later reclassified following court proceedings, the table shows the revised figures. The figures prior to 1996 are the best guide to recent trends. It can be seen that the number of homicides per million of the population are rare and have remained relatively stable since 1982. Over the last two decades, the *total* number of offences *currently recorded* as homicide are: (1976-1985) 5083, average 508 per annum; and (1986-1995) 5856, average 586 per annum (ref (a), p84).

How many mentally ill people commit homicide?

This is a question that is frequently asked, particularly by the media in response to cases of homicide committed by people who have been in contact with the mental health services within the preceding twelve months or so. Attempting to establish a precise number of homicides carried out by mentally ill people, however, is complex. Not until the recent establishment of the National Confidential Inquiry (ref (e)) has the information been collated and analysed in a particular way, and which therefore promises to deliver statistics which are more reliable than have ever been published before.

There are two obvious sources of data from the criminal statistics published by the Home Office and which can be readily drawn upon to provide a partial response. It is proposed here to present a brief analysis of these statistics, partly to draw out data which can be used with some degree of confidence, and partly to explore areas which are more problematic. The two Home Office sources are, first, the apparent circumstances surrounding the homicide, and, second, convictions of section 2 manslaughter under the Homicide Act 1957 (for definition of section 2 manslaughter, see end of paper). These data will be presented in turn.

There are difficulties with terminology in these statistics since the terms 'mental disorder' and 'mental disturbance' are used as defining categories. People suffering from a mental illness will account for the majority but not all of the instances in these categories. Similarly, 'section 2 manslaughter' figures are often taken to indicate mentally ill defendants but this will not always be the case. In this discussion, the above categories will be taken broadly to indicate the numbers of mentally ill people involved but it will be seen that it is not possible to ascertain exact figures.

Apparent circumstances of homicide

The apparent circumstances surrounding incidents of homicide are recorded in the statistics. Over the last decade, 'quarrel, revenge or loss of temper' reportedly accounted for more than half of all homicides and in more than half of the cases the suspect was known to the victim. Two categories of those recorded have direct relevance to the mentally ill. Table 2 shows the numbers of offences where the principal suspect committed suicide or appeared to be mentally disturbed.

TABLE 2 : NUMBER OF OFFENCES CURRENTLY RECORDED AS HOMICIDE WHERE THE PRINCIPAL SUSPECT COMMITTED SUICIDE OR WAS MENTALLY DISTURBED (1986-1996) (% of *cases currently recorded as homicide* appear in brackets) (ref. (a), p89-90)

Apparent circumstances	*1986#*	*1987*	*1988*	*1989*	*1990*	*1991*	*1992*	*1993*	*1994*	*1995*	*1996**
Suspect committed suicide	46 (8)	58 (10)	43 (8)	35 (7)	35 (6)	51 (8)	39 (7)	30 (5)	42 (7)	..	..
Suspect mentally disturbed	42 (7)	23 (4)	20 (4)	28 (5)	34 (6)	19 (3)	12 (2)	34 (6)	46 (7)	37 (6)	27 (4)
Total homicides**	563	599	547	524	555	623	581	566	635	663	627

**provisional figures only*
*** currently recorded as homicides*
#1986 figures taken from Home Office Criminal statistics England and Wales 1995, p80,81

It can be seen that the percentage of people in both groups (figures in brackets) has remained fairly constant over the years. Home Office Criminal Statistics state that 'Homicides where the suspect appeared to be mentally disturbed, and where there was no apparent motive, comprised 4% of homicides in 1996. This was a similar figure to previous years, although lower than in 1993-1995.' (ref. (a), p81). The statistics collected, however, do not enable an examination of the number of people with mental illness who may have been included in other circumstance categories, such as circumstances of revenge or loss of temper. Similarly, there is no information regarding the suspects who committed suicide following the homicide. This group constitutes 5-10% of suspects for homicide. Given the high rate of suicide among people with mental illness in comparison with the general population, it seems highly likely that some, if not a significant proportion, of these people would have been suffering from a mental illness.

Section 2 manslaughter figures

Table 3 shows the numbers of *convictions* for homicide from 1986-1996.

TABLE 3: CONVICTIONS FOR HOMICIDE 1986-1996 (% of the total number of *convictions* appear in brackets) (ref. (a), p92)

Convictions for homicide	*1986*	*1987*	*1988*	*1989*	*1990*	*1991*	*1992*	*1993*	*1994*	*1995*	*1996**
Murder	208 (41)	215 (42)	189 (38)	198 (31)	186 (42)	196 (39)	214 (43)	224 (45)	226 (46)	249 (48)	*144 (47)*
Section 2 Manslaughter	84 (17)	78 (15)	74 (15)	83 (13)	70 (16)	76 (15)	78 (16)	62 (12)	68 (14)	54 (10)	*34 (11)*
Other manslaughter	211 (42)	220 (43)	221 (45)	176 (28)	183 (41)	223 (45)	204 (41)	207 (42)	191 (39)	213 (41)	*127 (41)*
Infanticide	3 (1)	1 (0)	8 (1)	1 (0)	4 (1)	5 (1)	6 (1)	5 (1)	3 (0)	2 (0)	*3 (0)*
Total	506	514	492	458	443	500	502	498	488	518	*308*

**provisional figures only, 321 suspects for whom court proceedings were not completed by 1 August 1997*

Table 3 indicates that from 1986-1995 the percentage of section 2 manslaughter convictions fell from 17% to 10%. This is a higher proportion of the homicides committed by the mentally ill than indicated in Table 2, where suspects appeared to be mentally disturbed. In line with the Table 2 figures however, the section 2 manslaughter figures do suggest that a stable and relatively small proportion of homicides are carried out by the mentally ill. As before, however, lack of detail in the statistics means that it is not clear how many mentally ill people are included in the 'murder', 'other manslaughter' and 'infanticide' categories. It should also be noted that numbers of convictions will be an undercount of the total number of homicides committed, as expressed every year in the number of cases currently recorded as homicide

In addition, Table 4 indicates that a very small number of suspects of homicide were not convicted on the basis of being found unfit to plead or not guilty by reason of insanity. These figures clearly represent people who would be categorised as mentally ill.

TABLE 4: SUSPECTS NOT CONVICTED ON THE BASIS OF BEING FOUND UNFIT TO PLEAD AND NOT GUILTY ON THE GROUNDS OF DIMINISHED RESPONSIBILITY (ref. (a), P84)

Suspects not convicted	*1986*	*1987*	*1988*	*1989*	*1990*	*1991*	*1992*	*1993*	*1994*	*1995*	*1996*
Found unfit to plead	2	2	-	5	-	-	2	-	6	3	1
Found not guilty by reason of insanity	1	-	-	2	1	2	3	1	-	1	-

Further information can be found in the Home Office statistical bulletins of mentally disordered offenders (refs. (b), (c) and (d)) which give data about the population detained in hospitals.

Restricted patients

Context:

Information is kept about admissions of restricted and unrestricted patients to hospitals. In the last decade, admissions of restricted patients to hospital have more than trebled, from 329 - 1,057 (ref. (b), p3, paragraph 4). Those diagnosed as having a mental illness (with or without other disorders) represented over 90% of all restricted patient admissions in 1996 (ref. (b), p3, paragraph 6). The numbers of prisoners transferred to hospital grew steadily between 1989 and 1994, but fell in 1995 before recovering somewhat in 1996. Between 1989 and 1994 the number of unsentenced or untried patients increased more than five-fold, from 98 to 956 and in 1995 represented 47% of all admissions (ref. (c), p3, paragraph 5). Conversely, the proportion of those held under hospital orders is falling (ref. (c), p4, paragraph 8). The largest group of restricted patients over the last decade had been convicted of, or charged with, acts of violence against the person, including murder (ref. (b), p5, figure 4).

Table 5 shows the number of restricted patients admitted for offences of violence against the person.

TABLE 5: RESTRICTED PATIENTS ADMITTED (1) TO HOSPITAL FOR OFFENCES OF VIOLENCE AGAINST THE PERSON (ref. (b), p15)

Offence	*1986*	*1987*	*1988*	*1989*	*1990*	*1991*	*1992*	*1993*	*1994*	*1995*	*1996*
Murder	27	42	34	38	46	68	72	84	77	87	69
Other homicide	37	44	46	45	52	52	44	43	46	48	35
Other violence (2)	116	137	130	127	180	197	301	373	380	290	288

Note (1): Patients can be admitted to hospital more than once during a year, for instance reflecting a change of legal category. Each event is included in the table so that the above figures are an over-estimate of the number of offences for which patients have been convicted or charged. If s.48 transfers and recalls were excluded from the homicide figures, they would reduce to: Murder: 33 in 1992, 39 in 1993 and 35 in 1994; Other homicide: 33 in 1992, 38 in 1993 and 43 in 1994 (ref. (d), p14, note 5).

Note (2): 'Other violence' includes 'attempted murder' and 'threats or conspiracy to murder'.

The number of admissions in the murder and other violence categories have increased significantly over the last decade. Given note (1) however, it is not clear to what extent the actual numbers of patients having committed these offences has increased. The figures also do not include people given unrestricted hospital orders who have committed homicide. This information is presented in Table 6.

TABLE 6: PEOPLE GIVEN UNRESTRICTED HOSPITAL ORDERS BY THE COURTS FOR OFFENCES OF VIOLENCE AGAINST THE PERSON (ref. (b), p23).

Offence	*1986*	*1987*	*1988*	*1989*	*1990*	*1991*	*1992*	*1993*	*1994*	*1995*	*1996*
Murder	-	-	-	-	-	-	-	-	-	-	-
Other homicide	9	6	8	12	9	9	16	12	4	5	14
Other violence	195	163	203	208	212	160	196	187	202	163	196
All Offences	665	683	750	756	789	730	717	670	763	649	717

To complicate the matter still further, many patients are transferred from the prison service both before and after sentencing. Table 7 below shows the numbers of restricted patients admitted to hospital by legal category for offences of violence against the person in 1996.

TABLE 7: RESTRICTED PATIENTS ADMITTED TO HOSPITAL BY LEGAL CATEGORY FOR OFFENCES OF VIOLENCE AGAINST THE PERSON IN 1996 (ref. (b), p11)

Offence	*Hospital order with restrictions*	*Transferred from Prison Service after sentence*	*Transferred from Prison Service before sentence*	*Recalled after conditional discharge*	*Transferred from Scotland, N. Ireland etc.*	*Unfit to plead*	*Not guilty by reason of insanity*	*All legal categories*
Murder	-	30	36*	2	-	-	1	69
Other homicide	23	4	-	7	-	-	1	35
Other violence	86	54	118	22	-	5	3	288

Table 7 illustrates that many patients are transferred from the prison service to hospital prior to sentencing. In these cases the offence that the patient is recorded under will be the original indicted offence. In homicide cases, this would almost always be for the offence of murder. The actual offence would not be established until the subsequent court case and very often restricted patients indicted for murder are convicted of ‘other homicide’. i.e. many of the 36* admissions under ‘murder’ who were transferred from prison before sentence would end up in the ‘other homicide’ group.

The table indicates that in 1996, 30 patients were sentenced for murder prior to admission, i.e. not section 2 manslaughter cases. As stated earlier, the number of hospital admissions in the murder category has increased in the last decade. However, note (1) (see p6) also applies which means that the number of 30 is an over-estimate of actual cases. This figure does, however, suggest that there are cases where people are convicted of murder and are later found to be mentally ill and transferred to hospital. This supports the earlier suggestion that the section 2 manslaughter cases do not represent the true number of mentally ill people involved.

Home Office figures : conclusion

- The figures in Tables 2 and 3 suggest that the number of suspects of homicides who appear to be mentally disturbed and the numbers convicted for section 2 manslaughter represent between 2-13% of all homicides. These figures have been regularly used to suggest that the number of homicides committed by the mentally ill are a relatively small proportion of the total and that the proportion has remained stable or decreased slightly over the years.

- The figures, however, fail to account for: those mentally ill people who commit suicide following the homicide, a group who represent 5-10% of all homicide suspects; those mentally ill people who are diagnosed following sentence and transferred from prison to hospital; those who plead guilty to murder; those who are included in the 'other homicide' category; those found unfit to plead; and those found not guilty on the grounds of insanity.

- The data on restricted patient admissions to hospital show that admissions under the category of 'murder' have increased in the last decade (Table 5). This increase may reflect the recent Government emphasis on the diversion of mentally disordered offenders from the criminal justice system to health and social services (Reed Report, 1994).

- It can, therefore, be concluded that the data that are currently collected and published by the Home Office are insufficiently detailed to ascertain the numbers of mentally ill people who commit homicide. The numbers convicted of section 2 manslaughter are an under-estimate of cases involving the mentally ill but it is not possible to establish either accurate figures or how these have changed over time.

The National Confidential Inquiry into Suicide and Homicide by People with Mental Illness

The National Confidential Inquiry into Suicide and Homicide by People with Mental Illness (NCI) is a large research undertaking which is based at the University of Manchester, having been previously directed from London. It is funded by the Department of Health and the Royal College of Psychiatrists and its work is reviewed by a multidisciplinary steering group. Its remit is to conduct a national audit of suicides and homicides by people who have a history of contact with mental health services, to make recommendations on clinical practice and policy, and to identify training needs for mental health staff. A full report is due to be published in the Spring of 1999.

The NCI published a progress report in December 1997, under the authorship of its Director, Professor Louis Appleby. For the purposes of this report by The Zito Trust, primary consideration will be given to what the NCI has to say about homicides.

It is essential to point out that the NCI is concerned with homicides committed by mentally ill people who have a history of contact with mental health services prior to the homicide. There are two distinct categories here, those who have had some contact with mental health services at some time, and those who have had contact from mental health services in the twelve months before the homicide.

The Progress Report

The progress report states that in the year from April 1996, 408 homicide convictions were notified to the NCI, and that this is not a complete year sample but amounts to 80-90% of the expected annual figure of 450-500 homicide convictions. A question immediately arises as to whether this estimate is accurate, given Home Office statistics already analysed (see, for example, tables 1 and 3 above for statistics of homicides *currently recorded* contrasted with the number of *convictions* for homicide). This question will be revisited later in this discussion.

The NCI progress report states that the sample of 408 homicide convictions represents an unselected consecutive case series of those convicted, irrespective of their mental health history. Courts files had been made available on 327 of the original 408 cases and psychiatric reports were achieved for 73% of these 327, i.e. 238 cases. The point is made that there is likely to be a slight over-representation of severe mental disorder in this final sample of 238 cases because reports are more likely to be used and retained in courts files when someone is charged with homicide who has a mental illness. Equally, less severe disorders, including substance abuse and personality disorder, are likely to be under-represented in the sample.

Psychiatric history

The NCI's progress report presents the following data on its sample of 238 cases:

- 17% (39) had symptoms of mental illness at the time of the offence
- 43% (102) had a mental disorder of some kind at the time of the offence, including alcohol and substance abuse
- 25% (59) had a history of contact with adult mental health services
- 12% (28) had contact with mental health services in the year before the homicide

Predicted annual figures

The NCI makes a prediction in its progress report, based on its incomplete sample of 408 cases, that there are 50 homicides (i.e. 12%) annually (and 1000 suicides) by mentally ill people who have been in contact with mental health services in the year before the homicide. The degree and extent of contact is not recorded. Table 8 is reproduced from the progress report (Ref (e), p5):

Identification of Inquiry Cases

	Suicide	Homicide
Number of individuals notified to the Inquiry in the 12 months from April 1996	4,053	408
Proportion known to be in contact with mental health services in the year before suicide/homicide	26%	12%
Predicted annual number of Inquiry cases in contact with services in the year before suicide/homicide	c. 1,000	c. 50

Source: National Confidential Inquiry into Suicide and Homicide by People with Mental Illness. Progress Report: Table 1

These predicted figures are based, in the case of homicides, on the number of cases notified to the NCI in the (less than) 12 months since April 1996 (408). If we take the total number of homicides committed by those suffering from a mental disorder of some kind, including alcohol and substance abuse, and personality disorder - the NCI's 43% - the annual predicted figure for homicides in this category rises to 175.

If we then take the NCI's estimated rate of 450-500 homicides a year, the respective annual figures become:

- 77-85 (17%) committed by people with symptoms of mental illness at the time of the offence
- 194-215 (43%) committed by people with a mental disorder of some kind, including alcohol/substance and/or personality disorder
- 113-125 (25%) committed by people known to have had a history of contact with adult mental health services
- 54-60 (12%) committed by people in contact with mental health services in the year before the homicide

As already stated, however, there is a question mark over the NCI's estimate of 450-500 homicides a year. Home Office homicide figures for the decade 1986 to 1995 are as follows (ref. (a)) :

number initially recorded as homicide	***number indicted***	***number convicted***	***number currently recorded as homicide***
6840	6678	4919	5856

It will be observed that there are significant differences between the four categories. The category most often relied upon - the number convicted - is the lowest of all of them. A more accurate picture is provided, it is suggested here, if we consider the number of homicides per annum to lie *within the range* of the total for the number convicted (4919) and the total number currently recorded as homicide (5856), for the most accurate figure must lie somewhere in this range. This conclusion complies with guidance on the interpretation of homicide statistics published by the Home Office:

'Taking as a guide the more complete figures for the past six years (1990-1995) [4223], around 14 per cent of deaths intially recorded as homicides in 1996 [681] may be reclassified [586]. For the rest, around three quarters will result in conviction, there will be no suspect for around 13 per cent and for 1 in 10, court proceedings will not be initiated or will be concluded without conviction or acquittal, e.g. because the suspect died or committed suicide, or because proceedings were discontinued, or not initiated.' (ref. (a), p.80, para 4.4)

Taking the figures for 1995 (ref. (a), pp.84, 92), the number of homicides committed lies between the range of 518 (number convicted) and 663 (number currently recorded).

Applying NCI rates to this arrange, we have the following figures for homicides committed every year by people with mental illness or mental disorder:

- 88-113 (17%) reported to have had symptoms of mental illness at the time of the offence
- 223-318 (43%) suffering from mental disorder of some kind, including alcohol/substance abuse and/or personality disorder
- 130-166 (25%) known to have had a history of contact with adult mental health services
- 62-80 (12%) reported to have been in contact with mental health services in the year before the homicide

These figures are speculative but are based on evidence emerging from the official sources studied. A clearer clinical picture of these cases, with improved data, will become available, it is hoped, when the NCI publishes a full report in 1999.

Definition : Section 2 Manslaughter : Homicide Act 1957

Section 2 of the Homicide Act 1957 states that 'where a person kills or is party to the killing of another, he shall not be convicted of murder if he was suffering from such abnormality of mind (whether arising from a condition of arrested or retarded development of mind or any inherent causes or induced by disease or injury) as substantially impaired his mental responsibility for his acts or omissions in doing or being party to the killing' (cited in Prins, 1995, p25).

References

a) Home Office Criminal Statistics: England and Wales 1996. *Statistics Relating to Crime and Criminal Proceedings for the Year 1995.* The Home Office Research and Statistics Directorate. London: The Stationery Office.

b) Home Office Statistical Bulletin: *Statistics of Mentally Disordered Offenders England and Wales 1996.* (C. Kershaw & G. Renshaw) Issue 20/97. Research and Statistics Directorate: London.

c) Home Office Statistical Bulletin: *Statistics of Mentally Disordered Offenders England and Wales 1995.* (C. Kershaw & G. Renshaw) Issue 20/96. Research and Statistics Directorate: London.

d) Home Office Statistical Bulletin: *Statistics of Mentally Disordered Offenders England and Wales 1994.* Issue 20/95. Research and Statistics Directorate: London.

e) The National Confidential Inquiry (1997) *The National Confidential Inquiry into Suicide and Homicide by People with Mental Illness: Progress Report.* London: Department of Health.

Prins, H. (1995) *Offenders, Deviants or Patients?* 2nd Ed. Routledge: New York

Reed, J. (1994) *Report of the Working Group on High Security and Related Psychiatric Provision.* Department of Health: London.

CHAPTER SEVEN

MENTAL ILLNESS AND VIOLENT BEHAVIOUR
A SUMMARY OF CURRENT THINKING

Introduction

This chapter summarises the research that has taken place, particularly over the last ten to fifteen years, into the relationship between mental illness and violence. The term mental illness is used, in the main, to refer to schizophrenia. A more substantial report devoted to this subject will be published by The Zito Trust early in 1999. The purpose of this summary, which cannot be divorced from the complex issue of severely mentally ill patients who do not take their medication, is to render some degree of much needed clarity about a subject that we recognise is both highly sensitive, and which exposes organisations and individuals engaged in commentary on this issue, and prepared to say the unsayable, to criticism. The usual criticism is, of course, that any reference to, or observation about, the relationship between mental illness and violence not only stigmatises the mentally ill but alarms the general public, thereby reinforcing the stigma. Many of the voluntary sector organisations representing the mentally ill are quick to raise the spectre of stigma and public alarm whenever difficult topics such as dangerousness, violence, risk, treatment without consent, and other issues, are discussed, and they generally point to some of the more lurid and sensational media coverage as solid evidence of how the general public's views about the mentally ill are formed.

The evidence we have, however, suggests that the general public should be given more credit for its ability to transcend sensationalist newspaper reporting, absorb evidence, reflect upon it, and then form a balanced and coherent view. Our discussion of the poll carried out by MORI in 1997 about public attitudes to schizophrenia and community care (see Introduction) demonstrate that the general public's views about people who suffer from schizophrenia, and what should happen to them, are enlightened and sensitive. That their views about community care and schizophrenia should have become *more* enlightened, and *more* patient-orientated since 1990, when a similar poll was conducted, since when there has been media interest and coverage of community care failures and their consequences on an unprecedented scale, must give rise to some discomfort in those who would have us believe otherwise.

Christopher Clunis

Before summarising recent research on mental illness and violence, it is appropriate to set this rather academic overview in some kind of human context, particularly in the light of some of the observations just made.

Christopher Clunis has quickly acquired the questionable reputation of being one of the country's most famous psychiatric, community care patients. It was his killing of Jonathan Zito in December 1992 which, with Ben Silcock entering the lions' den at London Zoo just two weeks later, raised initial concerns at the Department of Health, culminating in a review of mental health policy published in August 1993 and subsequently known as the 'ten point plan'. This was followed by the publication in February 1994 of the Clunis report (Ritchie et al. 1994).

Christopher Clunis killed Jonathan Zito at Finsbury Park tube station in the afternoon of 17 December 1992. He stabbed Jonathan Zito three times in the face, from behind, in a completely unprovoked attack which was witnessed by about 75 passengers waiting for a train. The independent inquiry report described the care and treatment of Clunis as a catalogue of failure and missed opportunity. The care Clunis received was ineffectual in that it (a) did not keep him well, and (b) did not keep the public safe.

Between 1987 and 1993 Clunis was admitted to at least 12 hospitals, with several visits to the same hospitals. He was referred to three different social services departments and was seen by a total of some 45 doctors. As Professor Jeremy Coid put it (Coid, 1994):

'He also lived in one bail hostel, two rehabilitation hostels, two hostels for the homeless and six separate bed and breakfast accommodations. The geographical pattern of his movements are of considerable interest. He crossed the River Thames from one side of the city to another on four occasions, either by chance or deliberate placement, and with additional sideways moves between different in-patient and aftercare services. He meanwhile passed through three out of the four former Thames Regional Health Authorities.'

Professor Coid goes on to reiterate the inquiry report's observation that there are many more people like Clunis living in the community all over the country who are at risk to themselves or other people. Clunis was not some kind of freak patient and Jonathan Zito wasn't simply 'in the wrong place at the wrong time' - an unintelligent cliche which, even if it were true, could not possibly justify or validate the preceding 'catalogue of failure and missed opportunity'. Since the publication of the Clunis report in 1994 there have been a further 32 independent homicide inquiry reports published under health service guidelines, in England alone, with (at 1 March 1998) another 24 inquiry panels sitting.

As we have shown in chapter 4, many of these homicides have been committed by patients like Clunis, for whom services were totally inadequate.

The assessment of violence in the Clunis case

The Clunis report drew attention to many failures in the provision of care and after-care. Chief among these was the failure to assess Clunis' past history of violence or his propensity for violence in the future. Incidents of violence were repeatedly overlooked or minimised. The following are just some examples:

- as an inpatient, argumentative, irritable and threatening violence; pushes a patient so hard they are thrown across the floor. Discharged the following day
- violent incident in 1989 when police have to wrestle a knife from Clunis; not charge with any offence, so incident thereafter minimalised
- as an inpatient, stabbed another patient five times while he was in bed; police not called
- in a hostel, tries to gouge out fellow resident's eye
- in another hostel, chasing residents with a carving knife
- in hospital, aggressive and threatening to staff; given 'chemical strait-jacket'

- arrested for stabbing hostel resident and charged with grievous bodily harm with intent; medical evidence sought is not supplied, so case is dropped

- prison health care centre, Clunis hits duty solicitor and tries to hit the doctor

- in the community, Clunis tries to hit his GP, so is removed from the GP's list

- one week before the death of Jonathan Zito, Clunis is brandishing a screwdriver, attacks a man in the street and punches him in the face; police reluctant to act

- two days before the death of Jonathan Zito, Clunis chases two boys in a car park with the screwdriver

- 17 December 1992, Clunis kills Jonathan Zito by stabbing him in the eye three times

What can the recent research tell us about patients like Clunis?

Mental illness and violence : summary of research

Schizophrenia affects about 1 per cent of the adult population. The causes of it range from social labelling/abuse of power through to damage to the developing foetal brain. Whatever its causes, the condition is disabling and, for those who suffer from severe forms of schizophrenia, devastating. It affects the quality of life of sufferers who experience, to varying degrees, a range of positive and negative symptoms, which are often alleviated and exacerbated at the same time by treatment with antipsychotic medication, particularly by the conventional drugs such as chlorpromazine (largactil). Schizophrenia certainly affects the capacity of many sufferers to have intimate relationships, exercise ordinary life skills or gain meaningful employment. The financial cost of schizophrenia to the health service is described elsewhere in this report (see chapter 8). The personal cost, to sufferers, their families and carers, is often overlooked, as is the trend for many sufferers to become homeless and dependent on alcohol and/or drugs, or, as in one in every ten cases, to commit suicide.

During the early 1980s, there was a clear agreement among those working in the mental health field that there was no evidence to suggest that people suffering from mental illness were any more likely to commit acts of violence, or other criminal acts, than anyone else in the general population. This consenus was supported by research from academics pre-

Denmark (Hodgins,

of 538 cases, and

tus of 1241 men
non-fatal violent
9 out of 121
r offence

done most to
n an earlier
iolence were
tive violence
phrenia and

ontact with
bourhood.
lationship

of Link
lusions
cluster
else),
, and
ding
for
for
ing
er-
ct
ia

n, 1983; Hafner & Boker, 1982) This is,
mmentators on mental health policy.

ies of the relationship between mental illness and
ses more recent research which no longer supports
this important article.

hich has occurred among most researchers, and many
e refers to Monahan (1992), who has 'now shifted his
siders that to continue "to deny that mental disorder and
ated is disingenuous and ultimately counter productive".'
noting that 'contrary to findings of earlier research, an
ist between mental illness and the likelihood of being involved

ake people change their minds on this subject?

re cited by Mullen and, in an earlier article, by Hodgins (1994), which
ne view that there is a clear correlation between mental illness and
studies are summarised as follows:

- al. (1986) looked at disturbed and threatening behaviour in patients with nia in the month prior to their first admission and found that 19% had behaved in a which put the safety of others at risk
- er and McNeil (1988) reported even higher rates of violent behaviour, with 26% of those nitted have been violent within the previous six months, and a further 36% behaving in a ightening manner
- Klassen and O'Connor (1988) followed up 304 male patients, selected as at high risk of committing violence on the basis of past histories, and found that 25-30% were violent in the year following discharge
- Lindqvist and Allebeck (1990) followed 644 inpatients in Stockholm county for 14 years, all of them with a diagnosis of schizophrenia who were born between 1920 and 1959 and discharged in 1971. They found rates of offending among this group to be four times higher than among the general population
- Hodgins (1992) found a four-fold increase in the risk of conviction for offences involving violence among severely mentally men taken from a Swedish birth cohort study (and an even

greater risk for females), a finding which was confirmed in a second study in
1996)

- Wessely et al. (1994) used data from the Camberwell case register, a study
noted a three-fold increase in the risk of offending

- Taylor and Gunn (1984) carried out an important study of the psychiatric sta
remanded to Brixton Prison. They discovered that 9% of those convicted of
crimes and 11% convicted of fatal violence had schizophrenia, and that onl
psychotic offenders were without positive psychiatric symptoms at the time of the

- Swanson et al. (1990), in a study which is described by Mullen (1997) as havin
shift opinion in the USA, reanalysed data on over 10,000 subjects fro
Epidemiological Catchment Area Study, for whom self-reported levels of v
available. Twelve per cent of those diagnosed as schizophrenic reported assaulta
(cf. 2.4% of the general population). For those with the dual diagnosis of schiz
alcohol or substance abuse the rate rose to 25%

- Link et al. (1992, 1994) studied a sample of 375 patients currently or previously in c
the mental health services and a control group drawn from the same New York neigl
Their study was more sophisticated than others like it and they found 'a significant r
between violent behaviour and active symptoms' (Mullen, 1997)

- Taylor and Monahan (1996), in an overview of the literature, emphasise the significanc
et al's research into delusions and their association with violence, stating that those c
'most likely to be associated with delusional drive and violent offending were the relatec
of passivity delusions (beliefs about being under the control of something or someon
religious delusions, delusions of paranormal influence, and delusions of physical influenc
go on to add that 'the relation between violence and other psychotic symptoms, inc
hallucinations, is not impressive.' Taylor and Monahan's paper is important not on
drawing important attention to this association but for their observations about recent cal
new legal powers to bind unwilling patients into treatment, on both sides of the Atlantic, wa
that alternative and more robust procedures for community treatment may well prove cou
productive by increasing hospitalisation. Powers already exist under the Mental Health
1983 to detain a patient compulsorily in the interests of his own health, notwithstanding crit
for dangerousness.

- Eronen et al. (1996) studied all 1,423 homicides committed in Finland over a twelve year peri
and found that males with a primary diagnosis of schizophrenia were six times more likely to ki
than the general population of males, while the rate for females was five times. When the
diagnosis was schizophrenia and alcoholism, the respective rates rose to seventeen times for
males and eighty-five times for females.

- Taylor et al. (1998) analysed a record survey of all 1740 patients resident in the three special
hospitals between 1 January and 30 June 1993, most of whom had a criminal record, and found
that schizophrenia was most commonly associated with personal violence, with more than 75%
of those with a psychosis recorded as being driven to offend by their delusions. In their
conclusions, the authors state that '[f]or people with a pure psychosis, as symptoms were usually
a factor driving the index offence, treatment appears as important for public safety as for
personal health.'

Mental illness, violence and substance abuse

On the issue of substance abuse, mental illness and violence, Taylor et al. (1998) point to studies which have found that substance abuse is a 'significant and important factor which increases the risk that a person with a mental disorder will be violent' (eg Swanson et al, 1990; Taylor, 1993) and to the current under-estimation of substance abuse and its importance in this field. There is little evidence that the courts pay much attention to the role of substance abuse in offending behaviour, more often finding it unacceptable as a defence or in mitigation. There is an urgent need, highlighted by Alcohol Concern Ward and Applin, 1998), to play much closer attention to substance abuse, particularly on admission to hospital. 'Failure to do so', say Taylor et al. (1998) 'could lead to serious under-estimates of treatment need and of potential risk on return to the community.'

Mental illness and weapon carrying

In a recent article in *Psychiatric Bulletin*, Perry et al. (1998) describe the results of a study of 25 patients living in the community respresenting a wide range in terms of age, severity and length of illness. None had a history of learning disability or violent offending behaviour. Of the original 25, two declined to participate in the study, leaving a sample of 23. Six of the sample (23%) admitted to carrying a weapon while unwell at some stage of their illness. The weapons they carried included four knives, one cosh and a screwdriver. It was found that in all cases none of the patients had carried weapons before the onset of their illness. Home Office statistics on homicides committed in 1996 (Home Office, 1997) show that, overall, the most common method of killing is with a sharp instrument (32%).

Perry et al's study points to an increase in weapon carrying by the general population, particularly young males, and acknowledge it is difficult to draw conclusions from a small sample of 23 patients. What is significant, however, is the importance of the role of psychotic phenomena in the carrying of weapons. The study refers to research by Wessely et al. (1993), Taylor (1985) and Link and Stueve (1994), which provides evidence for the link between persecutory delusions and violent offending. This concept of 'rationality within irrationality' suggests that a patient suffering from (irrational) delusions may respond ‘rationally’ by protecting himself against those delusions, experienced as reality, by carrying a weapon.

Perry et al. feel ‘that the carrying of weapons should be incorporated into any standardised clinical risk assessment’ and that ‘[f]urther work needs to be done on the prevalence of this practice in larger populations.’

Conclusion

In concluding her summary review of the research on schizophrenia and violence, Hodgins (1994) makes the following important observations from the evidence discussed:

‘(1) Mental health programmes developed and implemented in the early 1960s which involved closing psychiatric hospitals and treating persons suffering from major mental disorders with neuroleptic medications in the community are overall a failure. A new policy for the treatment of persons suffering from schizophrenia must be developed in light of the real needs of these individuals and their rights and taking account of public safety. (2) Mental health professionals must be provided with the new evidence indicating the prevalence of aggressive behaviour and criminality among persons with major disorders. In addition, they must be trained to routinely assess the likelihood of a patient assaulting another. (3) It is time to begin seriously about how to prevent disorders such as schizophrenia.’

References

Binder, R.L. and McNeil D.E. (1988) ‘Effects of diagnosis and context on dangerousness’. *American Journal of Psychiatry*, 145: 728-32.

Coid, J. (1996) ‘Dangerous patients with mental illness: increased risks warrant new policies, adequate resources, and appropriate legislation’. *British Medical Journal*, 312: 965-9.

Eronen, M., Tihonen, J. and Hakola, P. (1996) ‘Schizophrenia and homicidal behaviour’. *Schizophrenia Bulletin*, 22: 83-9.

Hafner, H and Boker, W. (1988) *Crimes of violence by mentally abnormal offenders*. Cambridge: Cambridge University Press.

Hodgins, S. (1992) ‘Mental disorder, intellectual deficiency and crime: evidence from a birth cohort’. *Archives of General Psychiatry*, 49: 476-83.

Hodgins, S. (1994) ‘Schizophrenia and Violence: are new mental health policies needed?’ *Journal of Forensic Psychiatry*, 5: 473-77.

Hodgins, S., Mednick, S.A., Brennan, P.A., Schulsinger, F. and Engberg, M. (1996) 'Mental disorder and crime: evidence from a Danish birth cohort'. *Archives of General Psychiatry*, 53: 489-96.

Home Office. (1997) *Criminal statistics England and Wales 1996*. London: The Stationery Office.

Johnston, E., Crow, T., Johnson, A. and Macmillan, F. (1986) 'The Northwick Park Study of first episodes of schizophrenia. 1: Presentation of the illness and problems relating to admission'. *British Journal of Psychiatry*, 149: 51-6.

Klassen, D. and O'Connor, W.A. (1988) 'A prospective study of predictors of violence in adult male mental health admissions'. *Law and Human Behaviour*, 12: 143-158.

Lindqvist, P. and Allebeck, P. (1990) 'Schizophrenia and crime. A longitudinal follow-up of 644 schizophrenics in Stockholm'. *British Journal of Psychiatry*, 157: 345-50.

Link, B., Andrews, H. and Cullen, F. (1992) 'The violent and illegal behaviour of mental patients reconsidered'. *American Sociological Review*, 57: 275-92.

Link, B. G. and Stueve, A. (1994) 'Psychotic symptoms and the violent/illegal behaviour of mental patients compared to community controls'. In Monahan, J. and Steadman, H.J. (eds) *Violence and mental disorder*. Chicago: University of Chicago Press.

Monahan, J. and Steadman, H. (1983) 'Crime and mental illness: an epidemiological approach'. In Morris, N. and Tonry, M. (eds) *Crime and justice* (Vol. 4). Chicago: University of Chicago Press.

Monahan, J. (1992) 'Mental disorder and violent behaviour: perceptions and evidence'. *American Psychologist*, 47: 511-21.

Mullen, P.E. (1997) 'A reassessment of the link between mental disorder and violent behaviour, and its implications for clinical practice'. *Australian and New Zealand Journal of Psychiatry*, 31: 3-11.

Mulvey, E.P. (1994) 'Assessing the evidence of a link between mental illness and violence'. *Hospital and Community Psychiatry*, 45: 663-68.

Perry, D.W., Cormack, I.D., Campbell, C. and Reed, A. (1998) 'Weapon carrying: an important part of risk assessment'. *Psychiatric Bulletin*, 22: 92-3.

Ritchie, J., Dick, D. and Lingham, R. (1994) *The Report of the Inquiry into the Care and Treatment of Christopher Clunis*. London: HMSO.

Swanson, J., Holzer, C., Ganja, V and Jono, R. (1990) 'Violence and psychiatric disorder in the community: evidence from the Epidemiologic Catchment Area Surveys'. *Hospital and Community Psychiatry*, 41: 761-70.

Taylor, P.J. and Gunn, J. (1984) 'Violence and psychosis: 1. Risk of violence among psychotic men'. *British Medical Journal*, 288: 1945-9.

Taylor, P.J. (1985) 'Motives for offending among violent and psychotic men'. *British Journal of Psychiatry*, 147: 491-8.

Taylor, P.J., Grounds, A. and Snowden, P. (1993) 'Forensic Psychiatry in the National Health Service of England and Wales'. In Gunn, J and Taylor, P.J. (eds) *Forensic Psychiatry: Clinical, Legal and Ethical Issues*. Oxford: Butterworth-Heinemann.

Taylor, P.J. and Monahan, J. (1996) 'Commentary: Dangerous patients or dangerous diseases?' *British Medical Journal*, 312: 967-9.

Taylor, P.J., Leese, M., Williams, D., Butwell, M., Daly, R. and Larkin, E. (1998) 'Mental disorder and violence'. *British Journal of Psychiatry*, 172: 218-26.

Ward, M. and Applin, C. (1998) *The Unlearned Lesson: The Role of Alcohol and Drug Misuse in Homicides Perpetrated by People with Mental Health Problems*. London: Wynne Howard Books.

Wessely, S.C., Buchanan, A., Reed, A., Cutting, J., Everitt, B. and Garety, P. *et al.* (1993) 'Acting on delusions. I. Prevalence'. *British Journal of Psychiatry*, 163: 69-76.

Wessely, S.C., Castle, D., Douglas, A.J. and Taylor, P.J. (1994) 'The criminal careers of incident cases of schizophrenia'. *Psychological Medicine*, 24: 483-502.

CHAPTER EIGHT

THE IMPORTANCE OF MEDICATION IN THE TREATMENT OF SCHIZOPHRENIA

Introduction

The following discussion provides no more than an overview of the pharmaceutical industry's attempts to produce new and more efficacious antipsychotic compounds for the treatment of schizophrenia.

The treatment of schizophrenia places a great burden on the NHS, with the average cost of treatment per patient reaching some £2,138 per annum. Considering that over 185 thousand patients are receiving this type of treatment at any one time, the sums involved are vast - some £396 million - which represents 1.6 per cent of the total health care budget.

In all, after taking into account the cost of inpatient care, and community and personal health services, £16 billion is spent on the treatment of schizophrenia per year. It is imperative therefore, that the medications formulated are efficient and attractive to the patient, to ensure that the money spent on their production is not wasted.

To illustrate the scale of the problem: one in a hundred people suffer from schizophrenia, and there are roughly 15-30 new cases each year per 100,000 of the population. Thirty-five thousand patients enter hospital each year experiencing schizophrenia-related symptoms, and for every individual suffering schizophrenia, ten other people are affected by its consequences.

It is generally agreed in the medical profession that medication should start as soon as possible after onset of schizophrenia (as with illness generally), in order for it to have a beneficial effect. While one in ten schizophrenics who respond to medication remain permanently well, the other 90 per cent eventually relapse. When medication is continued for an indefinite period (maintenance therapy), the relapse rate is significantly reduced.

However, it is important to recognise that due to the nature of this illness, affected individuals are often out of touch with reality, lack insight and may not even be able to accept that they are ill, which decreases the likelihood that they will continue with their medication even if it is highly effective. This leads to the critical consideration of non-compliance, a factor present with all prescribed medication, but one of especial relevance with psychotic illness. As we have seen in chapters three and four, the nature of antipsychotic medication, with its often high side-effect profile, means that non-compliance is a serious consideration. It is estimated overall that 74 per cent of people suffering from schizophrenia who respond to medication will stop taking it within two years of discharge from hospital, with significant consequences for their own well-being and for the NHS and the community.

The development of antipsychotic compounds

The first treatment for schizophrenia came fifty years after the illness was first identified and isolated as a distinct mental illness. Chlorpromazine (largactil) was discovered by the pharmaceutical group Rhône-Poulenc Rorer. Derived from the drug phenothiazine, it was seen to be effective in calming the symptoms of the illness, but has a poor side-effect profile. The discovery of chlorpromazine led to the evolution of numerous other conventional compounds belonging to the same group, and over thirty of these are in use today. Each one, however, produces a high number of unwanted side-effects.

By 1958, Janssen Pharmaceuticals had formulated haloperidol, which is effective against the positive symptoms of schizophrenia. Haloperidol has a slightly better side-effect profile than chlorpromazine, causing fewer autonomic nervous system side-effects (for example, dry mouth and blurred vision), but the same extra pyramidal side-effects.

In the early 1960s, Sandoz (now Novartis) synthesised clozapine. Although not available in the UK until 1990, this development represented a breakthrough in treatment. Clozapine is effective in treating both the positive and negative symptoms of schizophrenia and has a relatively low side effect profile. It has the advantage over other compounds of being recommended for use in those patients who have not responded well to other types of antipsychotic treatment and represented a major step forward in the fight against the illness and against non-compliance.

How antipsychotics work

A basic operation of the brain is the transmission of messages. Put simply, this is done by messages being encrypted into impulses, which pass from nerve to nerve across the synapse (this is known as synaptic transmission). Several of the neurotransmitters which affect the transmission have been identified in the aetiology of schizophrenia, most notably dopamine and serotonin.

The so called 'dopamine hypothesis' as a biological causal explanation for schizophrenia has been in existence for many years now, and is based on the notion that schizophrenia results from overactivity of this neurotransmitter, rather in the way amphetamines can affect normal individuals (amphetamines increase the levels of dopamine in the brain).

It was also seen early on that drugs used in the treatment of Parkinson's disease induced hallucinations and delusions in recipients. Later it was found that these drugs stimulated dopamine receptors, and so dopamine became implicated with schizophrenic illness. A second association was made with the observation that a loss of dopamine-rich cells led to Parkinson's disease, which itself has symptoms very similar to the extrapyramidal symptoms caused in people treated with antipsychotic medication.

Research has shown that dopamine has several receptors in the brain, the main ones being the D2 and D3 receptors, and that drugs effective in the treatment of schizophrenia block the effects of dopamine at the receptor sites. On the basis of the dopamine hypothesis, therefore, it is possible to explain the positive symptoms of schizophrenia as resulting from overactivity of the dopamine system.

Serotonin (5HT) came to be associated with schizophrenia after it was seen that use of the illicit drug LSD could induce hallucinations. This drug was already known to mimic serotonin action and stimulate 5HT receptors, and thereby a second neurotransmitter came to be connected with the onset of schizophrenia. The three main receptors for serotonin are 5HT1, 5HT2 and 5HT3.

Conventional antipsychotics such as chlorpromazine and haloperidol work by having a high affinity with D2 receptors only, blocking their action and thereby reducing positive symptoms of schizophrenia but not the negative symptoms. Research now aims to produce antipsychotics which act on dopamine and serotonin receptors simultaneously, because such treatments have shown better overall responses in people with schizophrenia. Recent developments have focused on the development of atypical antipsychotics, that is compounds which combine dopamine and serotonin activity in one molecule (serotonin-dopamine antagonists).

Recent developments

At least six atypical antipsychotics have been launched in recent years, the best known among them being clozapine, the prototype atypical antipsychotic, so called due to its low side-effect profile and efficiency at alleviating symptoms. Risperidone was launched on the UK market in 1993, three years after clozapine became available. Risperidone acts on 5HT2 and D2 receptors, and is very successful in treating both the positive and negative symptoms of schizophrenia, and also has an improved side-effect profile.

Three other compounds launched since 1996 are sertindole, olanzapine and quetiapine, all of which are 5HT2 antagonists. Olanzapine acts on many different receptors, including D1, D2 and 5HT. Again, all three have have high efficacy with first onset schizophrenia with low side-effect profiles.

Towards the end of 1997, Lorex Synthelabo launched amisulpride in the UK. This Dopamine D2 and D3 antagonist has been available in France for some time. Ziprasidone should beome available during 1998.

These developments represent radical changes in the treatment of schizophrenia. These new, relatively non-toxic, compounds have a clinical profile in which extrapyramidal side-effects (tremor, rigidity, tardive dyskinesia, akathisia) are not usually seen at clinically effective doses. They are substantially more expensive than the conventional compounds like chlorpromazine, primarily because these conventional compounds are so cheap. In an era which emphasises caring for the patient in the community rather than in hospital, the new treatments are an important breakthrough after 30 years or so in which there have been few developments in this field and which should improve the well-being and quality of life of patients living in the community.

Tables 1-3 set out some of the details about the new atypical antispsychotics, contrasting them with more conventional compounds. One of the details to which attention is drawn is cost.

Is cost a factor in prescribing practices?

In 1996 the National Schizophrenia Fellowship (NSF) published the results of a survey of the experiences and views of psychiatrists of the new drugs available for the treatment of schizophrenia. The survey (Hogman, 1996) aimed to look not only at the influence of the cost of clozapine and risperidone on prescribing practices, contrasted with the cost of older antipsychotics (eg chlorpromazine), but also to look at psychiatrists' prescribing patterns of these two atypical antipsychotics. Developed in the 1960s, clozapine was not licensed in the UK until 1990. Patients prescribed clozapine are subject to a national blood monitoring programme due to the risk discovered in the 1970s of agranulocytosis (a disorder of white blood cells), which was fatal in some cases. Risperidone, launched in 1993, is most effective when prescribed for patients suffering their first onset of schizophrenia.

A maintenance dose of clozapine or risperidone costs in the region of £4 to £5.50 per day. A maintenance dose of chlorpromazine, with established high profile side-effects, costs about £0.08 per day. The difference in cost between the old style medication and the new atypical compounds is, therefore, substantial.

The NSF postal sample of 761 members of the social/community section of the Royal College of Psychiatrists (return rate = 59%) on precribing practices of clozapine and risperidone revealed some interesting, and worrying, results.

Table 1. NEW ATYPICAL ANTIPSYCHOTICS

DRUG NAME	BRAND NAME	DRUG COMPANY	DRUG TYPE	DRUG ACTION	LAUNCH DATE IN UK	PRICES	COST PER UNIT	TYPICAL MAINTENANCE DOSE
Clozapine	Clozaril	*Novartis (Formerly Sandoz)*	Dibenzo-diazepine	5HT and dopamine antagonist	1990	25mg. 28 tabs. - £12.52 25mg. 84 tabs.- £37.54 100mg. 28 tabs - £50.05 100mg. 84 tabs - £150.15	**£0.47** **£0.44** **£1.78** **£1.78**	150-300mg daily
Risperidone	Risperdal	*Janssen Cilag/Organon*	Benziso-xazole	5HT2 and dopamine D2 antagonist	1993	1mg. 6 tabs- £4.15 1mg. 20 tabs - £13.45 2mg. 60 tabs - £79.56 3mg. 60 tabs - £117.00 4mg. 60 tabs - £154.44	**£0.69** **£0.67** **£1.32** **£1.95** **£2.57**	4-8mg daily
Sertindole	Serdolect	*Lundbeck*	Phenylindole	5HT2 antagonist	1996	4mg. 30 tabs - £36.63 12mg. 28 tabs - £102.55 16mg. 28 tabs - £102.55 20mg. 28 tabs - £102.55	**£1.22** **£3.66** **£3.66** **£3.66**	12-20mg daily
Olanzapine	Zyprexa	*Lilly*	Thieno-benzodiazepine	D1, D2, 5HT2 and muscarin antagonist	1996	5mg. 28 tabs- £52.73 7.5mg. 56 tabs- £158.20 10mg. 28 tabs - £105.47 10mg. 56 tabs - £210.93	**£1.88** **£2.82** **£3.76** **£3.76**	12-20mg daily
Quetiapine	Seroquel	*Zeneca*		5HT2 antagonist	1997	25mg. 60 tabs-£28.50 100mg. 60 tabs-£113.10 200mg. 60 tabs-£113.10	**£0.48** **£1.86** **£1.86**	300-450mg daily

TABLE 2. CONVENTIONAL ANTIPSYCHOTICS

CATEGORY AND DRUG NAME	BRAND NAME	DRUG COMPANY	PRICE	COST PER UNIT [1]	TYPICAL MAINTENANCE DOSE
Aliphatic **Chlorpromazine**	Largactil	*Rhône-Poulenc Rorer*	10mg. 56 tablets - £0.39 25mg. 56 tablets - £0.54 50mg. 56 tablets - £2.10	**£0.01** **£0.01** **£0.04**	75-300mg daily
			10 x 2ml injection - £3.71 (25mg per ml)	**£0.37**	25-50mg single dose, followed by tablets
Methotrimeprazine	Nozinan	*Link*	25mg. 500 tablets - £75.00	**£0.15**	25-50mg daily
Promazine	Sparine	*Wyeth*	10 x 1ml injection - £2.59 (50mg per ml)	**£0.26**	50mg, 6- 8 hourly
Piperidines **Thiorizadine**	Melleril	*Sandoz*	10mg. 100 tablets - £1.10 25mg. 100 tablets - £1.81 50mg. 100 tablets - £3.51 100mg. 100 tablets-£6.78	**£0.01** **£0.01** **£0.04** **£0.07**	150-600mg daily
Pericyazine	Neulactil	*Rhône-Poulenc Rorer*	2.5mg. 84 tablets -£2.30 10mg. 84 tablets - £6.22	**£0.03** **£0.07**	15-75mg daily

[1] Per tablet/injection, to nearest penny.

TABLE 2. continued

CATEGORY AND DRUG NAME	BRAND NAME	DRUG COMPANY	PRICES	COST PER UNIT	TYPICAL MAINTENANCE DOSE
Piperazines **Perphanazine**	Fentazin	*Forley*	2mg. 100 tablets - £17.65 4mg. 100 tablets - £20.95	**£0.18** **£0.21**	12mg daily
Fluphenazine	Moditen	*Sanofi Winthrop*	1mg. 100 tablets - £5.30 2.5mg. 100 tablets -£6.63 5mg. 100 tablets - £8.87	**£0.05** **£0.07** **£0.09**	2.5-10mg daily
Trifluoperazine	Stelazine	*S.K. and F.*	1mg. 100 tablets - £2.78 5mg. 100 tablets - £3.97 2mg. 60 spansules[2] -£3.61 10mg. 30 spansules -£2.35 15mg. 30 spansules -£3.54	**£0.03** **£0.04** **£0.06** **£0.08** **£0.12**	15mg daily (approx.)
Prochlorperazine	Stemetil	*Rhône-Poulenc Rorer*	5mg. 84 tablets - £3.48 25mg. 56 tablets - £6.13 10 x 1ml injection - £3.83	**£0.04** **£0.11** **£0.38**	75-100mg daily 12.5-25mg daily, then switch to tablets

[2] Sustained release capsule.

TABLE 3. MISCELLANEOUS ANTIPSYCHOTICS

CATEGORY AND DRUG NAME	BRAND NAME	DRUG COMPANY	PRICE	COST PER UNIT	TYPICAL MAINTENANCE DOSE
Thioxanthenes **Zuclopenthixol**	Clopixol	*Lundbeck*	2mg. 100 tablets - £3.05 10mg. 100 tablets - £8.25 25mg. 100 tablets - £16.50 200mg/ml. 10 x 1ml injection -£32.25	**£0.03** **£0.08** **£0.16** **£3.23**	20-50mg daily 200-400mg every 2-4 weeks
Flupenthixol	Depixol	*Lundbeck*	3mg. 100 tablets - £14.25 20mg/ml.10 x 1ml injection - £15.53 20mg/ml.10 x 2ml injection - £25.99	**£0.14** **£1.55** **£2.60**	6-18mg daily 20-40mg every 2-4 weeks
Dibenzodiazepines **Clozapine**	Clozaril	*Novartis (Formerly Sandoz)*	25mg. 28 tablets - £12.52 25mg. 84 tablets - £37.54 100mg. 28 tablets - £50.75 100mg. 84 tablets -£150.15	**£0.45** **£0.45** **£1.81** **£1.79**	150-300mg daily
Loxapine	Loxapac	*Wyeth*	10mg. 100 tablets - £9.52 25mg. 100 tablets - £19.05 50mg. 100 tablets - £34.22	**£0.09** **£0.19** **£0.64**	60-100mg daily
Substituted benzamide **Sulpiride**	Dolmatil	*Delalande*	200mg. 100 tablets - £19.50 400mg. 100 tablets - £38.00	**£0.20** **£0.38**	200-1200mg daily
Depot butyrophenone **Haloperidol**	Haldol Decanoate	*Janssen-Cilag*	5mg. 100 tablets - £8.23 10mg. 100 tablets - £16.07 50mg/ml. 5 x 1ml injection - £21.75 100mg/ml. 5 x 1ml injection - £28.83	**£0.08** **£0.16** **£4.35** **£5.76**	5-10mg daily 50mg-300mg every 4 weeks
Diphenylbutylpipreridines **Pimozide**	Orap	*Sanofi Winthrop*	1mg. 100 tablets - £15.85 4mg. 100 tablets - £30.67 10mg. 100 tablets - £58.81	**£0.16** **£0.31** **£0.59**	Maximum 20mg daily

NSF findings

While risperidone was prescribed more often than clozapine, the majority of the sample had little experience with either compound and a significant number were clearly misinformed or unfamiliar with the profiles of these atypical antipsychotic treatments. A second major finding was that financial cost *is* an influential factor in decisions regarding the prescribing of these compounds. While it seems that health authority-driven formal rationing policies are rare (but not non-existent), informal policies and procedures are apparent, making prescribing powers less than clear cut. The NSF report concludes by recommending improved information and training about the new treatments for those who are prescribing them, and a ban on any form of rationing, whether formal or informal, by health authorities.

Conclusions

The development and marketing of new treatments in a climate of health service budget deficits raises obvious difficulties which are by no means confined to mental health services. Recent accounts of formal health authority bans on particular interventions (for example, for breast cancer, bowel cancer and new forms of chemotherapy) speak of treatment availability being dictated according to postcode (*Evening Standard*, 1997). Increasingly, we can expect such bans to be challenged in the courts, as in the case of the patient refused a new drug for the treatment of multiple sclerosis (at a prescription cost to the health authority of £10,000 per annum), the refusal being described in the High Court as 'disingenuous and unlawful', (*The Times*, 1997). Inevitably, it is only a matter of time before such a ban is challenged by a patient suffering from schizophrenia who is being required to take conventional medication with its known side-effects when new, atypical compounds are available with their much improved side-effect profile.

References

Evening Standard (1997) 'Postcode could cost you your life'. 14 July.

Hogman, G. (1996) *Is cost a factor? A survey by the National Schizophrenia Fellowship of the experiences and views of psychiatrists on new drugs for the treatment of schizophrenia.* London: National Schizophrenia Fellowship.

The Times (1997) 'Refusal to give MS victim new drug was illegal'. 12 July.

Appendix

Independent homicide inquiry reports published under HSG(94)27 since the Clunis report (February 1994)

HOMICIDE INQUIRY REPORT	DATE	COMMISSIONING AUTHORITY	CONTACT TELEPHONE
Christopher Clunis	24/02/94	North East Thames and South East Thames Regional Health Authorities	0171 7255300
Michael Buchanan	04/11/94	North West London Mental Health NHS Trust	0181 830 0033
Andrew Robinson (the Falling Shadow)	16/01/95	South Devon Health Authority	01803 866665
Ellen and Alan Boland*	01/03/95	North West London Mental Health NHS Trust	0181 830 0033
John Rous (Jonathan Newby)	26/07/95	Oxfordshire Health Authority	01865 741 741
Stephen Laudat (Woodley Team Report)	25/09/95	East London and The City Health Authority	0181 983 2900
Kenneth Grey (The Grey Report)	01/11/95	East London and The City Health Authority	0181 983 2900
Robert Viner* (The Viner Report)	12/03/96	Dorset Health Commission	01202 893 000
Jason Mitchell	27/03/96	Suffolk Health Authority	01473 323323
Nilesh Gadher	22/04/96	Ealing, Hammersmith and Hounslow Health Authority	0181 893 0303
Francis Hampshire	10/05/96	Redbridge and Waltham Forest Health Authority	0181 518 2299
Shaun Armstrong	13/06/96	Tees Health Authority	01642 320000
Raymond Sinclair	27/06/96	West Kent Health Authority	01622 710161
Kumbi Mabota	05/09/96	Redbridge and Waltham Forest Health Authority	0181 983 8000
Keith Taylor	26/09/96	Tees Health Authority	01642 320000
Richard John Burton	10/10/96	Leicestershire Health Authority	0116 273 1173
Anthony Smith	24/10/96	Southern Derbyshire Health Authority and Derbyshire County council	01332 626300
Richard Stoker	10/12/96	Northumberland Health Authority	01670 514 331
Martin Mursell	07/03/97	Camden and Islington Health Authority	0171 383 4155
Evan Barry	15/04/97	Bromley HA, South East London Probation Service, LB of Bromley	0181 315 8315
Darren Carr	05/06/97	Berkshire HA, Oxfordshire HA, Berkshire Social Services, Oxfordshire Social Services	0118 950 3094
Peter Winship	19/06/97	Nottingham Health Authority	0115 912 3344
Paul Smith	09/07/97	North West Anglia Health Authority	01733 882288
Gilbert Kopernik-Steckel*	15/07/97	Croyden Health Authority	0181 401 3900
Paul Medley	01/08/97	West Pennine Health Authority (Recommendations only published)	0161 455 5709
Doris Walsh	16/09/97	Coventry Health Authority	01203 552225
Sarah Beynon	21/10/97	Avon Health Authority	0117 976 6600
Michael Horner*	26/11/97	East Lancashire Health Authority	01282 619909
William Scott	04/12/97	Bedfordshire Health Authority	01582 744800
Damian Witts	10/12/97	Gloucestershire Health Authority	01452 318847
Norman Dunn	16/12/97	Newcastle and North Tyneside Health Authority	0191 2196000
James Stemp	18/12/97	Leicestershire Health Authority	0116 273 1173
Desmond Ledgester	12/01/98	Calderdale & Kirklees Health Authority	01484 466 000

(*defendant committed suicide)